The Terry Lectures

one world

Other volumes in the Terry Lecture Series available from Yale University Press

peter singer

one world

the ethics of globalization

yale university press   new haven & london

Published 2002 in the United States by Yale University Press and in Australia and New Zealand by Text Publishing.

Designed by Rebecca Gibb. Set in Adobe Garamond type by The Composing Room of Michigan, Inc. Printed in the United States of America by R.R. Donnelley & Sons.

A catalogue record for this book is available from the Library of Congress and the British Library.

ISBN 0-300-09686-0

The paper in this book meets the guidelines for permanence and durability of the Committee on Production Guidelines for Book Longevity of the Council on Library Resources.

10 9 8 7 6 5 4 3 2 1

The Dwight Harrington Terry Foundation Lectures on Religion in the Light of Science and Philosophy

The deed of gift declares that "the object of this foundation is not the promotion of scientific investigation and discovery, but rather the assimilation and interpretation of that which has been or shall be hereafter discovered, and its application to human welfare, especially by the building of the truths of science and philosophy into the structure of a broadened and purified religion. The founder believes that such a religion will greatly stimulate intelligent effort for the improvement of human conditions and the advancement of the race in strength and excellence of character. To this end it is desired that a series of lectures be given by men eminent in their respective departments, on ethics, the history of civilization and religion, biblical research, all sciences and branches of knowledge which have an important bearing on the subject, all the great laws of nature, especially of evolution . . . also such interpretations of literature and sociology as are in accord with the spirit of this foundation, to the end that the Christian spirit may be nurtured in the fullest light of the world's knowledge and that mankind may be helped to attain its highest possible welfare and happiness upon this earth." The present work constitutes the latest volume published on this foundation.

contents

preface

The core of this book is the Dwight H. Terry Lectures, which I gave at Yale University in November 2000. During what now seem like the tranquil and secure days of the first eight months of 2001, I filled in the gaps in the argument and wrote a complete draft. Then came September 11, and the title *One World* suddenly sounded a discord against the resonating talk of the "clash of civilizations." Nevertheless, the terrorist attack on that day, and America's response to it, confirms rather than denies the idea of a world that is increasingly becoming one, for it shows that no country, however mighty, is invulnerable to deadly force from the far corners of the earth. An American administration that had previously shown little concern for the opinion of the rest of the world found itself in need of the cooperation of other nations in a global campaign against terrorism. So the original title has remained, standing both as a description of the increasing interconnectedness of life on this planet, and as a prescription of what the basic unit for our ethical thinking should be.

I thank, first, the Dwight H. Terry Lecture Committee (Robert Adams, Robert Apfel, Radley Daly, Carlos Eire, Leo Hickey, John Ryden, Dianne Witte, and Richard Wood) for their invitation to give the lectures on which this book is based. My original idea was to use the opportunity to revisit the ethical issue of what people living in affluent nations ought to do for those in dire poverty elsewhere in the world. I thought that the Terry Lectures would provide a suitable occasion for responding to some criticisms of the approach I have taken to this topic since first writing about it in 1972. As I began to plan the lectures, however, I saw that the underlying issue—the extent to which we should take all humans, or even all sentient beings, as the basic unit of concern for our ethical thinking—has important implications for a much wider set of issues than foreign aid. I therefore devoted each of the four Terry Lectures to a different issue: climate change, the World Trade Organization and the globalization of trade, national sovereignty and humanitarian intervention, and the original topic of what the rich ought to do for the poor.

The audience at Yale provided me with the first sounding board for the material that developed into this book. I was fortunate to receive more detailed scrutiny and assistance from a group of wonderfully knowledgeable and helpful friends and colleagues. I owe a special debt of gratitude to Paula Casal, who read an entire draft, and even more than one version of some chapters. Her perceptive comments were just what an author needs: critical, sometimes sharply so, but always constructive. Brent Howard also read it all and gave me a superb set of comments that has made the book significantly better than it would otherwise have been. On climate change I learned an immense amount from Dale Jamieson, who generously shared with me his knowledge of both the science and the associated ethical and political issues. A series of seminars in the Science, Technology and the Environment Program at Princeton, led by David Bradford, gave me the chance to hear a wide variety of views on climate change and what we ought to do about it from scientists, economists, and people in industry. Matt Ball read the climate change chapter and challenged my lack of attention to the issue of the costs and benefits of trying to do something to mitigate climate change. I tried out a draft of this chapter at Princeton University's Political Philosophy Colloquium, from which I received useful feedback. I am especially grateful to Lawrence Mead, who subsequently took the trouble to put his comments in writing.

Thomas Pogge, Darryl McLeod, and Alex Gosseries gave me valuable comments on the chapter on the global economy. Branko Milanovic kindly corresponded with me about his research on problems in measuring global inequality. Vivian Leven sent me information about the implications of WTO decisions for animal welfare. Klaus Schwab, chair of the World Economic Forum, invited me to the 2000 meeting of that organization in Davos.

Chapter 4, on issues of national sovereignty and humanitarian intervention, was the basis for an Amnesty Lecture at Oxford in February 2001, a work-in-progress meeting of the faculty and fellows of the University Center for Human Values at Princeton, and a talk at the Graduate Center of the City University of New York. Each of these occasions brought many helpful comments. At Oxford I recall especially those of John Broome, Nick Owen, and Nir Eyal. At Princeton Leif Wenar responded, and his incisive comments led me to make many changes in the text. I also thank Michael Doyle and Gareth Evans for finding time to read the chapter and to give me the benefit of their practical experience with these issues. Stephen Macedo kept me informed on the work of the Princeton Project on Universal Jurisdiction, which he chairs, and Jonathan Marks provided further useful comments.

Earlier versions of chapter 5, on global affluence and poverty, were presented at a seminar in the Program for Ethics and Public Affairs at Princeton's Center for Human Values, as a Wesson Lecture at Stanford University, and to the Global Justice Conference held at Columbia Law School, New York, in March 2001. Thanks to Lori Gruen, Peter Godfrey-Smith, and Andy Kuper for their comments on those occasions. Invitations from Bernardo Kliksberg to speak at conferences of the Inter-American Development Bank, in Washington D.C. and Caracas, gave me a chance to get responses from those working in development. As I was completing this book, Matt Frazier was writing his senior thesis on development issues under my supervision, and I'm sure that I learned as much from him as he did from me. On ideas of citizenship, Melissa Williams provided me with some useful references. But in this area my greatest debt is to Thomas Pogge, both for valuable discussions and for sending me, prior to publication, the typescript of his important new book, *World Poverty and Human Rights.*

Jean Thomson Black, my contact at Yale University Press throughout the publication process, has been consistently helpful and supportive. I am also grateful to the three anonymous readers for the Press, each of whom made valuable suggestions, and to Margaret Otzel, whose careful copyediting saved me from several infelicities and errors, while allowing my favorite idiosyncrasies to remain.

This is the first book I have written since coming to Princeton University in 1999. The University as a whole, and the University Center for Human Values in particular, have provided ideal conditions for research and writing. Amy Gutmann, George Kateb, and Stephen Macedo have all, at various times during the writing of this book, served as Director of the Center, and I thank them for their support. Students in my Practical Ethics course have been a critical audience for some of the material in this book.

Aaron Jackson and Diego von Vacano have given excellent research assistance. Kim Girman, my assistant, has cheerfully and efficiently completed the many tasks I have given her. Finally, I thank Renata, my wife. Her readiness for adventure made it possible for us to leave our friends and families in Australia to try the new life in the United States, of which this book is one outcome; and her love and companionship have made that life such a positive experience.

1 a changing world

Consider two aspects of globalization: first, planes exploding as they slam into the World Trade Center, and second, the emission of carbon dioxide from the exhausts of gas-guzzling sport utility vehicles. One brought instant death and left unforgettable images that were watched on television screens all over the world; the other makes a contribution to climate change that can be detected only by scientific instruments. Yet both are indications of the way in which we are now one world, and the more subtle changes to which sport utility vehicle owners unintentionally contribute will almost certainly kill far more people than the highly visible one. When people in rich nations switch to vehicles that use more fuel than the cars they used to drive, they contribute to changes in the climate of Mozambique or Bangladesh —changes that may cause crops to fail, sea levels to rise, and tropical diseases to spread. As scientists pile up the evidence that continuing greenhouse gas emissions will imperil millions of lives, the leader of the nation that emits the largest share of these gases has said: "We will not do anything that harms our economy, because first things first are the people who live in America."[1] Consistently with this approach, as sales of sport utility vehicles increase, the average gas mileage of cars sold in the United States falls, and each year the U.S. Congress rejects measures to raise fuel efficiency standards for cars and trucks. The last time federal standards were raised was in 1985.[2]

President George W. Bush's remarks were not an aberration, but an expression of an ethical view that he has held for some time. In the second presidential debate against Vice-President Gore, then-Governor Bush was asked what use he would make of America's power and influence in the world. He said that he would use it for the benefit of all Americans. He may have learned this ethic from his father. The first President George Bush had said much the same thing at the 1992 Earth Summit in Rio de Janeiro. When representatives of developing nations asked Bush senior to put on the agenda the over-consumption of resources by the developed countries, especially the United States, he said "the American lifestyle is not up for negotiation." It was not negotiable, apparently, even if maintaining this lifestyle will lead to the deaths of millions of people subject to increasingly unpredictable weather and the loss of land used by tens of millions more people because of rising ocean levels and local flooding.[3]

But it is not only the two Bush administrations that have put the interests of Americans first. When it came to the crunch in the Balkans, the Clinton-Gore administration made it very clear that it was not prepared to risk the life of a single American in order to reduce the number of civilian casualties. In the context of the debate over whether to intervene in Bosnia to stop Serb "ethnic cleansing" operations directed against Bosnian Moslems, Colin Powell, then chairman of the Joint Chiefs of Staff, quoted with approval the remark of the nineteenth-century German statesman Otto von Bismarck, that all the Balkans were not worth the bones of a single one of his soldiers.[4] Bismarck, however, was not thinking of intervening in the Balkans to stop crimes against humanity. As Chancellor of Imperial Germany, he assumed that his country followed its national interest. To use his remark today as an argument against humanitarian intervention is to return to nineteenth-century power politics, ignoring both the bloody wars that style of politics brought about in the first half of the twentieth century, and the efforts of the second half of the twentieth century to find a better foundation for peace and the prevention of crimes against humanity.

In Kosovo, though the policy of giving absolute priority to American lives did not prevent intervention to defend the Kosovars, it led to the restriction of intervention to aerial bombardment. This strategy was a total success: NATO forces suffered not a single casualty in combat. Approximately 300 Kosovar, 209 Serb, and 3 Chinese civilians were killed. Observing the American policy, Timothy Garton Ash wrote: "It is a perverted moral code that will allow a million innocent civilians of another race to be made destitute because you are not prepared to risk the life of a single professional soldier of your own." This blunt condemnation of the approach to the duties of a national leader taken by—at least —the last three American presidents forces us to consider a fundamental ethical issue. To what extent should political leaders see their role narrowly, in terms of promoting the interests of their citizens, and to what extent should they be concerned with the welfare of people everywhere?

Romano Prodi, at the time President of the Commission of the European Union, and a former Prime Minister of Italy, responded to President George W. Bush's "first things first" statement by saying that "if one wants to be a world leader, one must know how to look after the entire earth and not only American industry." But the question is not only one for those who aspire to be world leaders. The leaders of smaller nations must also consider, in contexts like global warming, trade pacts, foreign aid, and the treatment of refugees, to what extent they are prepared to consider the interests of "outsiders."

As Ash suggests, there is a strong ethical case for saying that it is wrong for leaders to give absolute priority to the interests of their own citizens. The value of the life of an innocent human being does not vary according to nationality. But, it might be said, the abstract ethical idea that all humans are entitled to equal consideration cannot govern the duties of a political leader. Just as parents are expected to provide for the interests of their own children, rather than for the interests of strangers, so too in accepting the office of president of the United States, George W. Bush has taken on a specific role that makes it his duty to protect and further the interests of Americans. Other countries have their leaders, with similar roles in respect of the interests of their fellow citizens. There is no world political community, and as long as that situation prevails, we must have nation-states, and the leaders of those nation-states must give preference to the interests of their citizens. Otherwise, unless electors were suddenly to turn into altruists of a kind never before seen on a large scale, democracy could not function. American voters would not elect a president who gave no more weight to their interests than he or she gave to the interests of Bosnians or Afghans. Our leaders feel that they must give some degree of priority to the interests of their own citizens, and they are, so this argument runs, right to do so. But what does "some degree of priority" amount to, in practice?

Related to this question about the duties of national leaders is another one: Is the division of the world's people into sovereign nations a dominant and unalterable fact of life? Here our thinking has been affected by the horrors of Bosnia, Rwanda, and Kosovo. In Rwanda, a United Nations inquiry took the view that

2,500 military personnel, given the proper training and mandate, might have saved 800,000 lives.[5] Secretary-General Kofi Annan, who, as Under-Secretary-General for Peace-Keeping Operations at the time, must bear some responsibility for what the inquiry has termed a "terrible and humiliating" paralysis, has learned from this situation. Now he urges, "the world cannot stand aside when gross and systematic violations of human rights are taking place." What we need, he has said, are "legitimate and universal principles" on which we can base intervention.[6] This means a redefinition of state sovereignty, or more accurately, an abandonment of the absolute idea of state sovereignty that has prevailed in Europe since the Treaty of Westphalia in 1648.

The aftermath of the attacks on September 11, 2001 underlined in a very different way the extent to which our thinking about state sovereignty has changed over the past century. In the summer of 1914 another act of terrorism shocked the world: the assassination of the Austrian Crown Prince Franz Ferdinand and his wife in Sarajevo, by a Bosnian Serb nationalist. In the wake of that outrage Austria-Hungary presented an ultimatum to Serbia in which it laid out the evidence that the assassins were trained and armed by the Black Hand, a shadowy Serbian organization headed by the chief of Serbian military intelligence. The Black Hand was tolerated or supported by other Serbian government officials, and Serbian officials arranged safe passage across the border into Bosnia for the seven conspirators in the assassination plot.[7] Accordingly, Austria-Hungary's ultimatum demanded that the Serbs bring those responsible to justice and allow Austro-Hungarian officials to inspect the files to ensure that this had been done properly.

Despite the clear evidence of the involvement of Serbian officials in the crime—evidence that, historians agree, was substantially accurate—the ultimatum Austria-Hungary presented was widely condemned in Russia, France, Britain, and the United States. "The most formidable document I have ever seen addressed by one State to another that was independent," the British Foreign Minister, Sir Edward Grey, called it.[8] The American Legion's official history of the Great War used less diplomatic language, referring to the ultimatum as a "vicious document of unproven accusation and tyrannical demand."[9] Many historians studying the origins of the First World War have condemned the Austro-Hungarian ultimatum as demanding more than one sovereign nation may properly ask of another. They have added that the Austro-Hungarian refusal to negotiate after the Serbian government accepted many, but not all, of its demands, is further evidence that Austria-Hungary, together with its backer Germany, wanted an excuse to declare war on Serbia. Hence they must bear the guilt for the outbreak of the war and the nine million deaths that followed.

Now consider the American response to the terrorist attacks of September 11. The demands made of the Taliban by the Bush administration in 2001 were scarcely less stringent than those made by Austria-Hungary of Serbia in 1914. (The main difference is that the Austro-Hungarians insisted on the suppression of hostile nationalist propaganda. Freedom of speech was not so widely regarded, then, as a human right.) Moreover the American demand that the Taliban hand over Osama bin Laden was made without presenting to the Taliban any evidence at all linking him to the attacks of September 11. Yet the U.S. demands, far from being condemned as a mere pretext for aggressive war, were endorsed as reasonable and justifiable by a wide-ranging coalition of nations. When President Bush said, in speeches and press conferences after September 11, that he would not draw a distinction between terrorists and regimes that harbor terrorists, no ambassadors, foreign ministers, or United Nations representatives denounced this as a "vicious" doctrine or a "tyrannical" demand on other sovereign nations. The Security Council broadly endorsed it, in its resolution of September 28, 2001.[10] It seems that world leaders now accept that every nation has an obligation to every other nation of the world to suppress activities within its borders that might lead to terrorist attacks carried out in other countries, and that it is reasonable to go to war with a nation that does not do so. If Kaisers Franz Joseph I and Wilhelm II could see this, they might well feel that, since 1914, the world has come round to their view.

Shortly before the September 11 attacks, a United Nations panel issued a report pointing out that even if there were no altruistic concern among the rich nations to help the world's poor, their own self-interest should lead them to do so:

> In the global village, someone else's poverty very soon
> becomes one's own problem: of lack of markets for one's
> products, illegal immigration, pollution, contagious
> disease, insecurity, fanaticism, terrorism.[11]

Terrorism has made our world an integrated community in a new and frightening way. Not merely the activities of our neighbors, but those of the inhabitants of the most remote mountain valleys of the farthest-flung countries of our planet, have become our business. We need to extend the reach of the criminal law there and to have the means to bring terrorists to justice without declaring war on an entire country in order to do it. For this we need a sound global system of criminal justice, so justice does not become the victim of national differences of opinion. We also need, though it will be far more difficult to achieve, a sense that we really are one community, that we are people who recognize not only the force of prohibitions against killing each other but also the pull of obligations to assist one another. This may not stop religious fanatics from carrying out suicide missions, but it will help to isolate them and reduce their support. It was not a co-incidence that just two weeks after September 11, conservative members of the U.S. Congress abandoned their opposition to the payment of $582 million in back dues that the United States owed to the United Nations.[12] Now that America was calling for the world to come to its aid to stamp out terrorism, it was apparent that America could no longer flout the rules of the global community to the extent that it had been doing before September 11.

We have lived with the idea of sovereign states for so long that they have come to be part of the background not only of diplomacy and public policy but also of ethics. Implicit in the term "globalization" rather than the older "internationalization" is the idea that we are moving beyond the era of growing ties between nations and are beginning to contemplate something beyond the existing conception of the nation-state. But this change needs to be reflected in all levels of our thought, and especially in our thinking about ethics.

To see how much our thinking about ethics needs to change, consider the work that, better than any other, represents late-twentieth-century thinking on justice in the liberal American establishment: John Rawls's *A Theory of Justice.* When I first read this book, shortly after its publication in 1971, I was astonished that a book with that title, nearly 600 pages long, could utterly fail to discuss the injustice of the extremes of wealth and poverty that exist between different societies. Rawls's method (this is like mother's milk to every philosophy or politics student now) is to seek the nature of justice by asking what principles people would choose if they were choosing in conditions that prevented them from knowing what position they themselves would occupy. That is, they must choose without knowing whether they themselves would be rich or poor, a member of the dominant ethnic majority or of an ethnic minority, a religious believer or an atheist, highly skilled or unskilled, and so on. If we were to apply this method globally rather than for a given society, it would immediately be obvious that one fact about which those making the choice should be ignorant is whether they are citizens of a rich nation such as the United States or of a poor nation such as Haiti. In setting up his original choice, however, Rawls simply assumes that the people making the choice all belong to the same society and are choosing principles to achieve justice *within* their society. Hence when he argues that people choosing under the conditions he prescribes would choose a principle that, subject to constraints intended to protect equal liberty and fair equality of opportunity, seeks to improve the position of the worst-off, he limits the conception of "worst-off" to those within one's own society. If he accepted that to choose justly, people must also be ignorant of their citizenship, his theory would become a forceful argument for improving the prospects of the worst-off people in the world. But in the most influential work on justice written in twentieth-century America, this question *never even arises.*[13] Rawls does address it in his most recent book, *The Law of Peoples,* and I shall say something later about what he says there. His approach, however, remains firmly based on the idea that the unit for deciding what is just remains something like today's nation-state. Rawls's model is that of an international order, not a global order. This assumption needs reconsidering.

For most of the eons of human existence, people living only short distances apart might as well, for all the difference they made to each other's lives, have been living in separate worlds. A river, a mountain range, a stretch of forest or desert, a sea—these were enough to cut people off from each other. Over the past few centuries the isolation has dwindled, slowly at first, then with increasing rapidity. Now people living on opposite sides of the world are linked in ways previously unimaginable.

One hundred and fifty years ago, Karl Marx gave a one-sentence summary of his theory of history:

> The handmill gives you society with the feudal lord; the steam mill, society with the industrial capitalist.[14]

Today he could have added:

> The jet plane, the telephone, and the Internet give you a global society with the transnational corporation and the World Economic Forum.

Technology changes everything—that was Marx's claim, and if it was a dangerous half-truth, it was still an illuminating one. As technology has overcome distance, economic globalization has followed. In London supermarkets, fresh vegetables flown in from Kenya are offered for sale alongside those from nearby Kent. Planes bring illegal immigrants seeking to better their own lives in a country they have long admired. In the wrong hands the same planes become lethal weapons that bring down tall buildings. Instant digital communication spreads the nature of international trade from actual goods to skilled services. At the end of a day's trading, a bank based in New York may have its accounts balanced by clerks living in India. The increasing degree to which there is a single world economy is reflected in the development of new forms of global governance, the most controversial of which has been the World Trade Organization, but the WTO is not itself the creator of the global economy.

Global market forces provide incentives for every nation to put on what Thomas Friedman has called "a Golden Straitjacket," a set of policies that involve freeing up the private sector of the economy, shrinking the bureaucracy, keeping inflation low, and removing restrictions on foreign investment. If a country refuses to wear the Golden Straitjacket, or tries to take it off, then the electronic herd—the currency traders, stock and bond traders, and those who make investment decisions for multinational corporations—could gallop off in a different direction, taking with it the investment capital that countries want to keep their economy growing. When capital is internationally mobile, to raise your tax rates is to risk triggering a flight of capital to other countries with comparable investment prospects and lower taxation. The upshot is that as the economy grows and average incomes rise, the scope of politics may shrink—at least as long as no political party is prepared to challenge the assumption that global capitalism is the best economic system. When neither the government nor the opposition is prepared to take the risk of removing the Golden Straitjacket, the differences between the major political parties shrink to differences over minor ways in which the Straitjacket might be adjusted.[15] Thus even without the WTO, the growth of the global economy itself marks a decline in the power of the nation-state.

Marx argued that in the long run we never reject advances in the means by which we satisfy our material needs. Hence history is driven by the growth of productive forces. He would have been contemptuous of the suggestion that globalization is something foisted on the world by a conspiracy of corporate executives meeting in Switzerland, and he might have agreed with Thomas Friedman's remark that the most basic truth about globalization is *"No one is in charge."*[16] For Marx this is a statement that epitomizes humanity in a state of alienation, living in a world in which, instead of ruling ourselves, we are ruled by our own creation, the global economy. For Friedman, on the other hand, all that needs to be said about Marx's alternative—state control of the economy—is that *it doesn't work.*[17] (Whether there are alternatives to both capitalism and centrally controlled socialism that could work is another question, but not one for this book.)

Marx also believed that a society's ethic is a reflection of the economic structure to which its technology has given rise. Thus a feudal economy in which serfs are tied to their lord's land gives you the ethic of feudal chivalry based on the loyalty of knights and vassals to their lord, and the obligations of the lord to protect them in time of war. A capitalist economy requires a mobile labor force able to meet the needs of the market, so it breaks the tie between lord and vassal, substituting an ethic in which the right to buy and sell labor is paramount. Our newly interdependent global society, with its remarkable possibilities for linking people around the planet, gives us the material basis for a new ethic. Marx would have thought that such an ethic would serve the interests of the ruling class, that is, the rich nations and the transnational corporations they have spawned. But perhaps our ethics is related to our technology in a looser, less deterministic, way than Marx thought. Ethics appears to have developed from the behavior and feelings of social mammals. It became distinct from anything we can observe in our closest nonhuman relatives when we started using our reasoning abilities to justify our behavior to other members of our group. If the group to which we must justify ourselves is the tribe, or the nation, then our morality is likely to be tribal, or nationalistic. If, however, the revolution in communications has created a global audience, then we might feel a need to justify our behavior to the whole world. This change creates the material basis for a new ethic that will serve the interests of all those who live on this planet in a way that, despite much rhetoric, no previous ethic has ever done.[18]

If this appeal to our need for ethical justification appears to be based on too generous a view of human nature, there is another consideration of a very different kind that leads in the same direction. The great empires of the past, whether Persian, Roman, Chinese, or British, were, as long as their power lasted, able to keep their major cities safe from threatening barbarians on the frontiers of their far-flung realms. In the twenty-first century the greatest superpower in history was unable to keep the self-appointed warriors of a different world-view from attacking both its greatest city and its capital. The thesis of this book is that how well we come through the era of globalization (perhaps whether we come through it at all) will depend on how we respond ethically to the idea that we live in one world. For the rich nations not to take a global ethical viewpoint has long been seriously morally wrong. Now it is also, in the long term, a danger to their security.

2 one atmosphere

The Problem

There can be no clearer illustration of the need for human beings to act globally than the issues raised by the impact of human activity on our atmosphere. That we all share the same planet came to our attention in a particularly pressing way in the 1970s when scientists discovered that the use of chlorofluorocarbons (CFCs) threatens the ozone layer shielding the surface of our planet from the full force of the sun's ultraviolet radiation. Damage to that protective shield would cause cancer rates to rise sharply and could have other effects, for example, on the growth of algae. The threat was especially acute to the world's southernmost cities, since a large hole in the ozone was found to be opening up each year over Antarctica, but in the long term, the entire ozone shield was imperiled. Once the science was accepted, concerted international action followed relatively rapidly with the signing of the Montreal Protocol in 1985. The developed countries phased out virtually all use of CFCs by 1999, and the developing countries, given a ten-year period of grace, are now moving toward the same goal.

Getting rid of CFCs has turned out to be just the curtain raiser: the main event is climate change, or global warming. Without belittling the pioneering achievement of those who brought about the Montreal Protocol, the problem was not so difficult, for CFCs can be replaced in all their uses at relatively little cost, and the solution to the problem is simply to stop producing them. Climate change is a very different matter.

The scientific evidence that human activities are changing the climate of our planet has been studied by a working group of the Intergovernmental Panel on Climate Change, or IPCC, an international scientific body intended to provide policymakers with an authoritative view of climate change and its causes. The group released its *Third Assessment Report* in 2001, building on earlier reports and incorporating new evidence accumulated over the previous five years. The Report is the work of 122 lead authors and 515 contributing authors, and the research on which it was based was reviewed by 337 experts. Like any scientific document it is open to criticism from other scientists, but it reflects a broad consensus of leading scientific opinion and is by far the most authoritative view at present available on what is happening to our climate.

The *Third Assessment Report* finds that our planet has shown clear signs of warming over the past century. The 1990s were the hottest decade, and 1998 the hottest year, recorded over the 140 years for which meteorological records have been kept. As 2001 drew to a close, the World Meteorological Organization announced that it would be second only to 1998 as the hottest year recorded. In fact nine of the ten hottest years during this period have occurred since 1990, and temperatures are now rising at three times the rate of the early 1900s.[1] Sea levels have risen by between 10 and 20 centimeters (4 to 8 inches) over the past century. Since the 1960s snow and ice cover has decreased by about 10 percent, and mountain glaciers are in retreat everywhere except near the poles. In the past three decades the El Niño effect in the southern hemisphere has become more intense, causing greater variation in rainfall. Paralleling these changes is an unprecedented increase in concentrations of carbon dioxide, methane, and nitrous oxide in the atmosphere, produced by human activities such as burning fossil fuels, the clearing of vegetation, and (in the case of methane) cattle and rice production. Not for at least 420,000 years has there been so much carbon dioxide and methane in the atmosphere.

How much of the change in climate has been produced by human activity, and how much can be explained by natural variation? The *Third Assessment Report* finds "new and stronger evidence that most of the warming observed over the last 50 years is attributable to human activities," and, more specifically, to greenhouse gas emissions. The report also finds it "very likely" that most of the rise in sea levels over the past century is due to global warming.[2] Those of us who have no expertise in the scientific aspects of assessing climate change and its causes can scarcely disregard the views held by the overwhelming majority of those who do possess that expertise. They could be wrong—the great majority of scientists sometimes are—but in view of what is at stake, to rely on that possibility would be a risky strategy.

What will happen if we continue to emit increasing amounts of greenhouse gases and global warming continues to accelerate? The *Third Assessment Report* estimates that between 1990 and 2100, average global temperatures will rise by at least 1.4°C (2.5°F), and perhaps by as much as 5.8°C (10.4°F).[3] Although these average figures may seem quite small—whether tomorrow is going to be 20°C (69°F) or 22°C (72°F) isn't such a big deal—

even a 1°C rise in average temperatures would be greater than any change that has occurred in a single century for the past 10,000 years. Moreover, some regional changes will be more extreme and are much more difficult to predict. Northern landmasses, especially North America and Central Asia, will warm more than the oceans or coastal regions. Precipitation will increase overall, but there will be sharp regional variations, with some areas that now receive adequate rainfall becoming arid. There will also be greater year-to-year fluctuations than at present—which means that droughts and floods will increase. The Asian summer monsoon is likely to become less reliable. It is possible that the changes could be enough to reach critical tipping points at which the weather systems alter or the directions of major ocean currents, such as the Gulf Stream, change.

What will the consequences be for humans?

- As oceans become warmer, hurricanes and tropical storms that are now largely confined to the tropics will move farther from the equator, hitting large urban areas that have not been built to cope with them. This is a prospect that is viewed with great concern in the insurance industry, which has already seen the cost of natural disasters rise dramatically in recent decades.[4]
- Tropical diseases will become more widespread.
- Food production will rise in some regions, especially in the high northern latitudes, and fall in others, including sub-Saharan Africa.
- Sea levels will rise by between 9 and 88 centimeters (between 4 and 35 inches).

Rich nations may, at considerable cost, be able to cope with these changes without enormous loss of life. They are in a better position to store food against the possibility of drought, to move people away from flooded areas, to fight the spread of disease-carrying insects and to build seawalls to keep out the rising seas. Poor nations will not be able to do so much. Bangladesh, the world's most densely populated large country, has the world's largest system of deltas and mudflats, where mighty rivers like the Ganges and the Brahmaputra reach the sea. The soil in these areas is fertile, but the hazards of living on such low-lying land are great. In 1991 a cyclone hit the coast of Bangladesh, coinciding with high tides that left 10 million people homeless and killed 139,000. Most of these people were living on mudflats in the deltas. People continue to live there in large numbers because they have nowhere else to go. But if sea levels continue to rise, many peasant farmers will have no land left. As many as 70 million people could be affected in Bangladesh, and a similar number in China. Millions more Egyptian farmers on the Nile delta also stand to lose their land. On a smaller scale, Pacific island nations that consist of low-lying atolls face even more drastic losses. Kiribati, placed just to the west of the International Date Line, was the first nation to enter the new millennium. Ironically, it may also be the first to leave it, disappearing beneath the waves. High tides are already causing erosion and polluting fragile sources of fresh water, and some uninhabited islands have been submerged.

Global warming would lead to an increase in summer deaths due to heat stress, but these would be offset by a reduced death toll from winter cold. Much more significant than either of these effects, however, would be the spread of tropical diseases, including diseases carried by insects that need warmth to survive. The *Third Assessment Report* considers several attempts to model the spread of diseases like malaria and dengue, but finds that the research methodology is, at this stage, inadequate to provide good estimates of the numbers likely to be affected.[5]

If the Asian monsoon becomes less reliable, hundreds of millions of peasant farmers in India and other countries will go hungry in the years in which the monsoon brings less rain than normal. They have no other way of obtaining the water needed for growing their crops. In general, less reliable rainfall patterns will cause immense hardship among the large proportion of the world's population who must grow their own food if they want to eat.

The consequences for non-human animals and for biodiversity will also be severe. In some regions plant and animal communities will gradually move farther from the equator, or to higher altitudes, following climate patterns. Elsewhere that option will not be available. Australia's unique alpine plants and animals already survive only on the country's highest alpine plains and peaks. If snow ceases to fall on their territory, they will become extinct. Coastal ecosystems will change dramatically, and warmer waters may destroy coral reefs. These predictions look ahead only as far as 2100, but even if greenhouse gas emissions have been stabilized by that time, changes in climate will persist for hundreds, perhaps thousands of years. A small change in average global temperatures could, over the next millennium, lead to the melting of the Greenland ice cap which, added to the partial melting of the West Antarctic ice sheet, could increase sea levels by 6 meters, or nearly 20 feet.[6]

All of this forces us to think differently about our ethics. Our value system evolved in circumstances in which the atmosphere, like the oceans, seemed an unlimited resource, and responsibilities and harms were generally clear and well defined. If someone hit someone else, it was clear who had done what. Now the twin problems of the ozone hole and of climate change have revealed bizarre new ways of killing people. By spraying deodorant at your armpit in your New York apartment, you could, if you use an aerosol spray propelled by CFCs, be contributing to the skin cancer deaths, many years later, of people living in Punta Arenas, Chile. By driving your car, you could be releasing carbon dioxide that is part of a causal chain leading to lethal floods in Bangladesh.[7] How can we adjust our ethics to take account of this new situation?

Rio and Kyoto

That seemingly harmless and trivial human actions can affect people in distant countries is just beginning to make a significant difference to the sovereignty of individual nations. Under existing international law, individuals and companies can sue for damages if they are harmed by pollution coming from another country, but nations cannot take other nations to court. In January 2002, Norway announced that that it would push for a binding international "polluter-pays" scheme for countries. The announcement followed evidence that Britain's Sellafield nuclear power plant is emitting radioactive wastes that are reaching the Norwegian coastline. Lobsters and other shellfish in the North Sea and the Irish Sea have high levels of radioactive technetium-99.[8]

The Sellafield case has revealed a gap in environmental legislation on a global basis. Norway is seeking an international convention on environmental pollution, first at the European level, and then, through the United Nations, globally. The principle is one that is difficult to argue against, but if Norway can force Britain to pay for the damage its leaking nuclear plant causes to their coastline, will not nations like Kiribati be able to sue America for allowing large quantities of carbon dioxide to be emitted into the atmosphere, causing rising sea levels to submerge their island homes? Although the link between rising sea levels and a nation's emissions of greenhouse gases is much more difficult to prove than the link between Britain's nuclear power plant and technetium-99 found along the Norwegian coast, it is hard to draw a clear line of principle between the two cases. Yet accepting the right of Kiribati to sue for damages for American greenhouse gas emissions makes us one world in a new and far more sweeping sense than we ever were before. It gives rise to a need for concerted international action.

Climate change entered the international political arena in 1988, when the United Nations Environment Program and the World Meteorological Office jointly set up the Intergovernmental Panel on Climate Change. In 1990 the IPCC reported that the threat of climate change was real, and a global treaty was needed to deal with it. The United Nations General Assembly resolved to proceed with such a treaty. The United Nations Framework Convention on Climate Change was agreed to in 1992, and opened for signature at the Earth Summit, or more formally, the United Nations Conference on Environment and Development, which was held in Rio de Janeiro in the same year. This "framework convention" has been accepted by 181 governments. It is, as its name suggests, no more than a framework for further action, but it calls for greenhouse gases to be stabilized at safe levels, and it says that the parties to the convention should do this "on the basis of equity and in accordance with their common but differentiated responsibilities and respective capabilities." Developed nations should "take the lead in combating climate change and the adverse effects thereof." The developed nations committed themselves to 1990 levels of emissions by the year 2000, but this commitment was not legally binding.[9] For the United States and several other countries, that was just as well, because they came nowhere near meeting it. In the United States, for example, by 2000 carbon dioxide emissions were 14 percent higher than they were in 1990. Nor was the trend improving, for the increase between 1999 and 2000 was 3.1 percent, the biggest one-year increase since the mid 1990s.[10]

The framework convention builds in what is sometimes called "the precautionary principle," calling on the parties to act to avoid the risk of serious and irreversible damage even in the absence of full scientific certainty. The convention also recognizes a "right to sustainable development," asserting that economic development is essential for addressing climate change. Accordingly, the Rio Earth Summit did not set any emissions reduction targets for developing countries to meet.

The framework convention set up a procedure for holding "conferences of the parties" to assess progress. In 1995, this conference decided that more binding targets were needed. The result, after two years of negotiations, was the 1997 Kyoto Protocol, which set targets for 39 developed nations to limit or reduce their greenhouse gas emissions by 2012. The limits and reductions were designed to reduce total emissions from the developed nations to a level at least 5 percent below 1990 levels. The national targets vary, however, with the European Union nations and the United States having targets of 8 percent and 7 percent, respectively, below 1990 levels, and other nations, such as Australia, being allowed to go over their 1990 levels. These targets were arrived at through negotiations with government leaders, and they were not based on any general principles of fairness, nor much else that can be defended on any terms other than the need to get agreement.[11] This was necessary since under the prevailing conception of national sovereignty, countries cannot be bound to meet their targets unless they decide to sign the treaty that commits them to do so. To assist countries in reaching their targets, the Kyoto Protocol accepted the principle of "emissions trading," by which one country can buy emissions credits from another country that can reach its target with something to spare.

The Kyoto conference did not settle the details of how countries could meet their targets, for example, whether they would be allowed credits for planting forests that soak up carbon dioxide from the atmosphere, and how emissions trading was to operate. After a meeting at The Hague failed to reach agreement on these matters, they were resolved at further meetings held in Bonn and Marrakech in July and November 2001, respectively. There, 178 nations reached an historic agreement that makes it possible to put the Kyoto Protocol into effect. American officials, however, were merely watching from the sidelines. The United States was no longer a party to the agreement.

The Kyoto agreement will not solve the problem of the impact of human activity on the world's climate. It will only slow the changes that are now occurring. For that reason, some skeptics have argued that the likely results do not justify the costs of putting the agreement into effect. In an article in *The Economist,* Bjorn Lomborg writes:

> Despite the intuition that something drastic needs to be done about such a costly problem, economic analyses clearly show that it will be far more expensive to cut carbon-dioxide emissions radically than to pay the costs of adaptation to the increased temperatures.[12]

Lomborg is right to raise the question of costs. It is conceivable, for example, that the resources the world is proposing to put into reducing greenhouse gas emissions could be better spent on increasing assistance to the world's poorest people, to help them develop economically and so cope better with climate change. But how likely is it that the rich nations would spend the money in this manner? As we shall see in Chapter 5, their past record is not encouraging. A comparatively inefficient way of helping the poor may be better than not helping them at all.

Significantly, Lomborg's highly controversial book, *The Skeptical Environmentalist,* offers a more nuanced picture than the bald statement quoted above. Lomborg himself points out that, even in a worst-case scenario in which Kyoto is implemented in an inefficient way, "there is no way that the cost will send us to the poorhouse." Indeed, he says, one could argue that whether we choose to implement the Kyoto Protocol or to go beyond it, and actually stabilize greenhouse gases:

> The total cost of managing global warming *ad infinitum* would be the same as deferring the [economic] growth curve by less than a year. In other words we would have to wait until 2051 to enjoy the prosperity we would otherwise have enjoyed in 2050. And by that time the average citizen of the world will have become twice as wealthy as she is now.[13]

Lomborg does claim that the Kyoto Protocol will lead to a net loss of $150 billion. This estimate assumes that there will be emissions trading within the developed nations, but not among all nations of the world. It also assumes that the developing nations will remain outside the Protocol—in which case the effect of the agreement will be only to delay, by a few years, the predicted changes to the climate. But if the developing nations join in once they see that the developed nations are serious about tackling their emissions, and if there is global emissions trading, then Lomborg's figures show that the Kyoto pact will bring a net benefit of $61 billion.

These estimates all assume that Lomborg's figures are sound—a questionable assumption, for how shall we price the increased deaths from tropical diseases and flooding that global warming will bring? How much should we pay to prevent the extinction of species and entire ecosystems? Even if we could answer these questions, and agree on the figures that Lomborg uses, we would still need to consider his decision to discount all future costs at an annual rate of 5 percent. A discount rate of 5 percent means that we consider losing $100 today to be the equivalent of losing $95 in a year's time, the equivalent of losing $90.25 in two years' time, and so on. Obviously, then, losing something in, say, 40 years' time isn't going to be worth much, and it wouldn't make sense to spend a lot now to make sure that you don't lose it. To be precise, at this discount rate, it would only be worth spending $14.20 to-day to make sure that you don't lose $100 in 40 years' time. Since the costs of reducing greenhouse gas emissions will come soon, whereas most of the costs of not doing anything to reduce them fall several decades into the future, this makes a huge difference to the cost/benefit equation. Assume that unchecked global warm-ing will lead to rising sea levels, flooding valuable land in 40 years' time. With an annual discount rate of 5 percent, it is worth spending only $14.20 to prevent flooding that will permanently inundate land worth $100. Losses that will occur a century or more hence dwindle to virtually nothing. This is not because of inflation—we are talking about costs expressed in dollars already adjusted for inflation. It is simply discounting the future. Lom-borg justifies the use of a discount rate by arguing that if we invest $14.20 today, we can get a (completely safe) return of 5 percent on it, and so it will grow to $100 in 40 years. Though the use of a dis-count rate is a standard economic practice, the decision about which rate should be used is highly speculative, and assuming different interest rates, or even acknowledging uncertainty about interest rates, would lead to very different cost/benefit ratios.[14] There is also an ethical issue about discounting the future. True, our investments may increase in value over time, and we will be-come richer, but the price we are prepared to pay to save human lives, or endangered species, may go up just as much. These val-ues are not consumer goods, like TVs or dishwashers, which drop in value in proportion to our earnings. They are things like health, something that the richer we get, the more we are willing to spend to preserve. An ethical, not an economic, justification would be needed for discounting suffering and death, or the extinction of species, simply because these losses will not occur for 40 years. No such justification has been offered.

It is important to see Kyoto not as the solution to the problem of climate change, but as the first step. It is reasonable to raise questions about whether the relatively minor delay in global warming that Kyoto would bring about is worth the cost. But if we see Kyoto as a necessary step for persuading the developing countries that they too should reduce greenhouse gas emissions, we can see why we should support it. Kyoto provides a platform from which a more far-reaching and also more equitable agreement can be reached. Now we need to ask what that agreement would need to be like to satisfy the requirement of equity or fairness.

What Is an Equitable Distribution?

In the second of the three televised debates held during the 2000 U.S. presidential election, the candidates were asked what they would do about global warming. George W. Bush said:

> I'll tell you one thing I'm not going to do is I'm not going to let the United States carry the burden for cleaning up the world's air, like the Kyoto treaty would have done. China and India were exempted from that treaty. I think we need to be more even-handed.

There are various principles of fairness that people often use to judge what is fair or "even-handed." In political philosophy, it is common to follow Robert Nozick in distinguishing between "historical" principles and "time-slice" principles.[15] An historical principle is one that says: we can't decide, merely by looking at the present situation, whether a given distribution of goods is just or unjust. We must also ask how the situation came about; we must know its history. Are the parties entitled, by an originally justifiable acquisition and a chain of legitimate transfers, to the holdings they now have? If so, the present distribution is just. If not, rectification or compensation will be needed to produce a just distribution. In contrast, a time-slice principle looks at the existing distribution at a particular moment and asks if that distribution satisfies some principles of fairness, irrespective of any preceding sequence of events. I shall look at both of these approaches in turn.

A Historical Principle: "The Polluter Pays" or "You Broke It, Now You Fix It"

Imagine that we live in a village in which everyone puts their wastes down a giant sink. No one quite knows what happens to the wastes after they go down the sink, but since they disappear and have no adverse impact on anyone, no one worries about it. Some people consume a lot, and so have a lot of waste, while others, with more limited means, have barely any, but the capacity of the sink to dispose of our wastes seems so limitless that no one worries about the difference. As long as that situation continues, it is reasonable to believe that, in putting waste down the sink, we are leaving "enough and as good" for others, because no matter how much we put down it, others can also put as much as they want, without the sink overflowing. This phrase "enough and as good" comes from John Locke's justification of private property in his *Second Treatise on Civil Government*, published in 1690. In that work Locke says that "the earth and all that is therein is given to men for the support and comfort of their being." The earth and its contents "belong to mankind in common." How, then, can there be private property? Because our labor is our own, and hence when we mix our own labor with the land and its products, we make them our own. But why does mixing my labor with the common property of all humankind mean that I have gained property in what belongs to all humankind, rather than lost property in my own labor? It has this effect, Locke says, as long as the appropriation of what is held in common does not prevent there being "enough and as good left in common for others."[16] Locke's justification of the acquisition of private property is the classic historical account of how property can be legitimately acquired, and it has served as the starting point for many more recent discussions. Its significance here is that, if it is valid and the sink is, or appears to be, of limitless capacity, it would justify allowing everyone to put what they want down the sink, even if some put much more than others down it.

Now imagine that conditions change, so that the sink's capacity to carry away our wastes is used up to the full, and there is already some unpleasant seepage that seems to be the result of the sink's being used too much. This seepage causes occasional problems. When the weather is warm, it smells. A nearby water hole where our children swim now has algae blooms that make it unusable. Several respected figures in the village warn that unless usage of the sink is cut down, all the village water supplies will be polluted. At this point, when we continue to throw our usual wastes down the sink we are no longer leaving "enough and as good" for others, and hence our right to unchecked waste disposal becomes questionable. For the sink belongs to us all in common, and by using it without restriction now, we are depriving others of their right to use the sink in the same way without bringing about results none of us wants. We have an example of the well-known "tragedy of the commons."[17] The use of the sink is a limited resource that needs to be shared in some equitable way. But how? A problem of distributive justice has arisen.

Think of the atmosphere as a giant global sink into which we can pour our waste gases. Then once we have used up the capacity of the atmosphere to absorb our gases without harmful consequences, it becomes impossible to justify our usage of this asset by the claim that we are leaving "enough and as good" for others. The atmosphere's capacity to absorb our gases has become a finite resource on which various parties have competing claims. The problem is to allocate those claims justly.

Are there any other arguments that justify taking something that has, for all of human history, belonged to human beings in common, and turning it into private property? Locke has a further argument, arguably inconsistent with his first argument, defending the continued unequal distribution of property even when there is no longer "enough and as good" for others. Comparing the situation of American Indians, where there is no private ownership of land, and hence the land is not cultivated, with that of England, where some landowners hold vast estates and many laborers have no land at all, Locke claims that "a king of a large and fruitful territory there [i.e., in America] feeds, lodges, and is clad worse than a day laborer in England."[18] Therefore, he suggests, even the landless laborer is better off because of the private, though unequal, appropriation of the common asset, and hence should consent to it. The factual basis of Locke's comparison between English laborers and American Indians is evidently dubious, as is its failure to consider other, more equitable ways of ensuring that the land is used productively. But even if the argument worked for the landless English laborer, we cannot defend the private appropriation of the global sink in the same way. The landless laborer who no longer has the opportunity to have a share of what was formerly owned in common should not complain, Locke seems to think, because he is better off than he would have been if inegalitarian private property in land had not been recognized. The parallel argument to this in relation to the use of the global sink would be that even the world's poorest people have benefited from the increased productivity that has come from the use of the global sink by the industrialized nations. But the argument does not work, because many of the world's poorest people, whose shares of the atmosphere's capacity have been appropriated by the industrialized nations, are not able to partake in the benefits of this increased productivity in the industrialized nations—they cannot afford to buy its products—and if rising sea levels inundate their farm lands, or cyclones destroy their homes, they will be much worse off than they would otherwise have been.

Apart from John Locke, the thinker most often quoted in justifying the right of the rich to their wealth is probably Adam Smith. Smith argued that the rich did not deprive the poor of their share of the world's wealth, because:

> The rich only select from the heap what is most precious
> and agreeable. They consume little more than the poor,
> and in spite of their natural selfishness and rapacity,
> though they mean only their own conveniency, though the
> sole end which they propose from the labours of all the
> thousands whom they employ, be the gratification of their
> own vain and insatiable desires, they divide with the poor
> the produce of all their improvements.[19]

How can this be? Because, Smith tells us, it is as if an "invisible hand" brings about a distribution of the necessaries of life that is "nearly the same" as it would have been if the world had been divided up equally among all its inhabitants. By that Smith means that in order to obtain what they want, the rich spread their wealth throughout the entire economy. But while Smith knew that the rich could be selfish and rapacious, he did not imagine that the rich could, far from consuming "little more" than the poor, consume many times as much of a scarce resource as the poor do. The average American, by driving a car, eating a diet rich in the products of industrialized farming, keeping cool in summer and warm in winter, and consuming products at a hitherto unknown rate, uses more than fifteen times as much of the global atmospheric sink as the average Indian. Thus Americans, along with Australians, Canadians, and to a lesser degree Europeans, effectively deprive those living in poor countries of the opportunity to develop along the lines that the rich ones themselves have taken. If the poor were to behave as the rich now do, global warming would accelerate and almost certainly bring widespread catastrophe.

The putatively historical grounds for justifying private property put forward by its most philosophically significant defenders—writing at a time when capitalism was only beginning its rise to dominance over the world's economy—cannot apply to the current use of the atmosphere. Neither Locke nor Smith provides any justification for the rich having more than their fair share of the finite capacity of the global atmospheric sink. In fact, just the contrary is true. Their arguments imply that this appropriation of a resource once common to all humankind is not justifiable. And since the wealth of the developed nations is inextricably tied to their prodigious use of carbon fuels (a use that began more than 200 years ago and continues unchecked today), it is a small step from here to the conclusion that the present global distribution of wealth is the result of the wrongful expropriation by a small fraction of the world's population of a resource that belongs to all human beings in common.

For those whose principles of justice focus on historical processes, a wrongful expropriation is grounds for rectification or compensation. What sort of rectification or compensation should take place in this situation?

One advantage of being married to someone whose hair is a different color or length from your own is that, when a clump of hair blocks the bath outlet, it's easy to tell whose hair it is. "Get your own hair out of the tub" is a fair and reasonable household rule. Can we, in the case of the atmosphere, trace back what share of responsibility for the blockage is due to which nations? It isn't as easy as looking at hair color, but a few years ago researchers measured world carbon emissions from 1950 to 1986 and found that the United States, with about 5 percent of the world's population at that time, was responsible for 30 percent of the cumulative emissions, whereas India, with 17 percent of the world's population, was responsible for less than 2 percent of the emissions.[20] It is as if, in a village of 20 people all using the same bathtub, one person had shed 30 percent of the hair blocking the drain hole and three people had shed virtually no hair at all. (A more accurate model would show that many more than three had shed virtually no hair at all. Indeed, many developing nations have per capita emissions even lower than India's.) In these circumstances, one basis of deciding who pays the bill for the plumber to clear out the drain would be to divide it up proportionately to the amount of hair from each person that has built up over the period that people have been using the tub, and has caused the present blockage.

There is a counterargument to the claim that the United States is responsible for more of the problem, per head of population, than any other country. The argument is that because the United States has planted so many trees in recent decades, it has actually soaked up more carbon dioxide than it has emitted.[21] But there are many problems with this argument. One is that the United

States has been able to reforest only because it earlier cut down much of its great forests, thus releasing the carbon into the atmosphere. As this suggests, much depends on the time period over which the calculation is made. If the period includes the era of cutting down the forests, then the United States comes out much worse than if it starts from the time in which the forest had been cut, but no reforestation had taken place. A second problem is that forest regrowth, while undoubtedly desirable, is not a long-term solution to the emissions problem but a temporary and one-shot expedient, locking up carbon only while the trees are growing. Once the forest is mature and an old tree dies and rots for every new tree that grows, the forest no longer soaks up significant amounts of carbon from the atmosphere.[22]

At present rates of emissions—even including emissions that come from changes in land use like clearing forests—contributions of the developing nations to the atmospheric stock of greenhouse gases will not equal the built-up contributions of the developed nations until about 2038. If we adjust this calculation for population—in other words, if we ask when the contributions of the developing nations per person will equal the per person contributions of the developed nations to the atmospheric stock of greenhouse gases—the answer is: not for at least another century.[23]

If the developed nations had had, during the past century, per capita emissions at the level of the developing nations, we would not today be facing a problem of climate change caused by human activity, and we would have an ample window of opportunity to do something about emissions before they reached a level sufficient to cause a problem. So, to put it in terms a child could understand, as far as the atmosphere is concerned, the developed nations broke it. If we believe that people should contribute to fixing something in proportion to their responsibility for break-

ing it, then the developed nations owe it to the rest of the world
to fix the problem with the atmosphere.

Time-Slice Principles

The historical view of fairness just outlined puts a heavy burden
on the developed nations. In their defense, it might be argued
that at the time when the developed nations put most of their cumulative contributions of greenhouse gases into the atmosphere,
they could not know of the limits to the capacity of the atmosphere to absorb those gases. It would therefore be fairer, it may
be claimed, to make a fresh start now and set standards that look
to the future, rather than to the past.

There can be circumstances in which we are right to wipe the
slate clean and start again. A case can be made for doing so with
respect to cumulative emissions that occurred before governments could reasonably be expected to know that these emissions
might harm people in other countries. (Although, even here, one
could argue that ignorance is no excuse and a stricter standard of
liability should prevail, especially since the developed nations
reaped the benefits of their early industrialization.) At least since
1990, however, when the Intergovernmental Panel on Climate
Change published its first report, solid evidence about the hazards associated with emissions has existed.[24] To wipe the slate
clean on what happened since 1990 seems unduly favorable to the
industrialized nations that have, despite that evidence, continued
to emit a disproportionate share of greenhouse gases. Nevertheless, in order to see whether there are widely held principles of
justice that do not impose such stringent requirements on the developed nations as the "polluter pays" principle, let us assume
that the poor nations generously overlook the past. We would
then need to look for a time-slice principle to decide how much
each nation should be allowed to emit.

An Equal Share for Everyone

If we begin by asking, "Why should anyone have a greater claim to part of the global atmospheric sink than any other?" then the first, and simplest response is: "No reason at all." In other words, everyone has the same claim to part of the atmospheric sink as everyone else. This kind of equality seems self-evidently fair, at least as a starting point for discussion, and perhaps, if no good reasons can be found for moving from it, as an end point as well.

If we take this view, then we need to ask how much carbon each country would be allowed to emit and compare that with what they are now emitting. The first question is what total level of carbon emission is acceptable. The Kyoto Protocol aimed to achieve a level for developed nations that was 5 percent below 1990 levels. Suppose that we focus on emissions for the entire planet and aim just to stabilize carbon emissions at their present levels. Then the allocation per person conveniently works out at about 1 metric ton per year. This therefore becomes the basic equitable entitlement for every human being on this planet.

Now compare actual per capita emissions for some key nations. The United States currently produces more than 5 tons of carbon per person per year. Japan and Western European nations have per capita emissions that range from 1.6 tons to 4.2 tons, with most below 3 tons. In the developing world, emissions average 0.6 tons per capita, with China at 0.76 and India at 0.29.[25] This means that to reach an "even-handed" per capita annual emission limit of 1 ton of carbon per person, India would be able to increase its carbon emissions to more than three times what they now are. China would be able to increase its emissions by a more modest 33 percent. The United States, on the other hand, would have to reduce its emissions to no more than one-fifth of present levels.

One objection to this approach is that allowing countries to have allocations based on the number of people they have gives them insufficient incentive to do anything about population growth. But if the global population increases, the per capita amount of carbon that each country is allocated will diminish, for the aim is to keep total carbon emissions below a given level. Therefore a nation that increases its population would be imposing additional burdens on other nations. Even nations with zero population growth would have to decrease their carbon outputs to meet the new, reduced per capita allocation.

By setting national allocations that are tied to a specified population, rather than allowing national allocations to rise with an increase in national population, we can meet this objection. We could fix the national allocation on the country's population in a given year, say 1990, or the year that the agreement comes into force. But since different countries have different proportions of young people about to reach reproductive age, this provision might produce greater hardship in those countries that have younger populations than in those that have older populations. To overcome this, the per capita allocation could be based on an estimate of a country's likely population at some given future date. For example, estimated population sizes for the next 50 years, which are already compiled by the United Nations, might be used.[26] Countries would then receive a reward in terms of an increased emission quota per citizen if they achieved a lower population than had been expected, and a penalty in terms of a reduced emission quota per citizen if they exceeded the population forecast—and there would be no impact on other countries.

Aiding the Worst-off

Giving everyone an equal share of a common resource like the capacity of the atmosphere to absorb our emissions is, I have argued, a fair starting point, a position that should prevail unless there are good reasons for moving from it. Are there such reasons? Some of the best-known accounts of fairness take the view that we should seek to improve the prospects of those who are worst off. Some hold that we should assist the worst-off only if their poverty is due to circumstances for which they are not responsible, like the family, or country, into which they were born, or the abilities they have inherited. Others think we should help the worst-off irrespective of how they have come to be so badly off. Among the various accounts that pay special attention to the situation of the worst-off, by far the most widely discussed is that of John Rawls. Rawls holds that, when we distribute goods, we can only justify giving more to those who are already well off if this will improve the position of those who are worst off. Otherwise, we should give only to those who are, in terms of resources, at the lowest level.[27] This approach allows us to depart from equality, but only when doing so helps the worst-off.

Whereas the strict egalitarian is vulnerable to the objection that equality can be achieved by "leveling down," that is, by bringing the rich down to the level of the poor without improving the position of the poor, Rawls's account is immune to this objection. For example, if allowing some entrepreneurs to become very rich will provide them with incentives to work hard and set up industries that provide employment for the worst-off, and there is no other way to provide that employment, then that inequality would be permissible.

That there are today very great differences in wealth and income between people living in different countries is glaringly obvious. It is equally evident that these differences depend largely on the fact that people are born into different circumstances, rather than because they have failed to take advantage of opportunities open to them. Hence if in distributing the atmosphere's capacity to absorb our waste gases without harmful consequences, we were to reject any distribution that fails to improve the situation of those who, through no fault of their own, are at the bottom of the heap, we would not allow the living standard in poor countries to be reduced while rich countries remain much better off.[28] To put this more concretely: if, to meet the limits set for the United States, taxes or other disincentives are used that go no further than providing incentives for Americans to drive more fuel-efficient cars, it would not be right to set limits on China that prevent the Chinese from driving cars at all.

In accordance with Rawls's principle, the only grounds on which one could argue against rich nations bearing *all* the costs of reducing emissions would be that to do so would make the poor nations even worse off than they would have been if the rich nations were not bearing all the costs. It is possible to interpret President George W. Bush's announcement of his administration's policy on climate change as an attempt to make this case. Bush said that his administration was adopting a "greenhouse gas intensity approach" which seeks to reduce the amount of greenhouse gases the United States emits per unit of economic activity. Although the target figure he mentioned—an 18 percent reduction over the next 10 years—sounds large, if the U.S. economy continues to grow as it has in the past, such a reduction in greenhouse gas intensity will not prevent an *increase* in the total quantity of greenhouse gases that the United States emits. But Bush justified this by saying "economic growth is the solution, not the problem" and "the United States wants to foster economic growth in the developing world, including the world's poorest nations."[29]

Allowing nations to emit in proportion to their economic activity—in effect, in proportion to their Gross Domestic Product—can be seen as encouraging efficiency, in the sense of leading to the lowest possible level of emissions for the amount produced. But it is also compatible with the United States continuing to emit more emissions, because it is producing more goods. That will mean that other nations must emit less, if catastrophic climate change is to be averted. Hence for Bush's "economic growth is the solution, not the problem" defense of a growth in U.S. emissions to succeed as a Rawlsian defense of continued inequality in per capita emissions, it would be necessary to show that United States production not only makes the world as a whole better off, but also makes the poorest nations better off than they would otherwise be.

The major ethical flaw in this argument is that the primary beneficiaries of U.S. production are the residents of the United States itself. The vast majority of the goods and services that the United States produces—89 percent of them—are consumed in the United States.[30] Even if we focus on the relatively small fraction of goods produced in the United States that are sold abroad, U.S. residents benefit from the employment that is created and, of course, U.S. producers receive payment for the goods they sell abroad. Many residents of other countries, especially the poorest countries, cannot afford to buy goods produced in the United States, and it isn't clear that they benefit from U.S. production.

The factual basis of the argument is also flawed: the United States does not produce more efficiently, in terms of greenhouse gas emissions, than other nations. Figures published by the U.S. Central Intelligence Agency show that the United States is well above average in the amount of emissions per head it produces in proportion to its per capita GDP. (See table on page 40.) On this basis the United States, Australia, Canada, Saudi Arabia, and Russia are relatively inefficient producers, whereas developing countries like India and China join European nations like Spain, France, and Switzerland in producing a given value of goods per head for a lower than average per capita level of emissions.[31]

Emissions and Gross Domestic Product

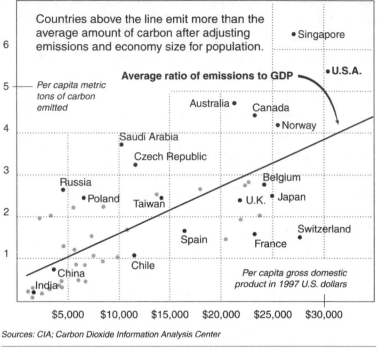

Countries above the line emit more than the average amount of carbon after adjusting emissions and economy size for population.

Average ratio of emissions to GDP

Per capita metric tons of carbon emitted

Singapore

U.S.A.

Australia

Canada

Norway

Saudi Arabia

Czech Republic

Russia

Belgium

Poland

Taiwan

U.K.

Japan

Spain

France

Switzerland

Chile

China

India

Per capita gross domestic product in 1997 U.S. dollars

$5,000 $10,000 $15,000 $20,000 $25,000 $30,000

Sources: CIA; Carbon Dioxide Information Analysis Center

Because the efficiency argument fails, we must conclude that a principle that requires us to distribute resources so as to improve the level of the worst-off would still, given the huge resource gap between rich and poor nations, make the rich nations bear all of the costs of the required changes.

The Greatest Happiness Principle

Classical utilitarians would not support any of the principles of fairness discussed so far. They would ask what proposal would lead to the greatest net happiness for all affected—net happiness being what you have left when you deduct the suffering caused from the happiness brought about. An advocate of preference utilitarianism, a more contemporary version of utilitarianism, would instead ask what proposal would lead to the greatest net satisfaction of preferences for all concerned. But in this context, the difference between the two forms of utilitarianism is not very significant. What is much more of a problem, for either of these views, is to indicate how one might do such a calculation. Evidently, there are good utilitarian reasons for capping the emission of greenhouse gases, but what way of doing it will lead to the greatest net benefits?

Perhaps it is because of the difficulty of answering such broad questions about utility that we have other principles, like the ones we have been discussing. They give you easier answers and are more likely to lead to an outcome that approximates the best consequences (or is at least as likely to do so as any calculation we could make without using those principles). The principles discussed above can be justified in utilitarian terms, although each for somewhat different reasons. To go through them in turn:

1. The principle that "the polluter pays," or more generally "you broke it, you fix it," provides a strong incentive to be careful about causing pollution, or breaking things. So if it is upheld as a general rule, there will be less pollution, and people will be more careful in situations where they might break something, all of which will be to the general benefit.

2. The egalitarian principle will not, in general, be what utilitarians with perfect knowledge of all the consequences of their actions would choose. Where there is no other clear criterion for allocating shares, however, it can be an ideal compromise that leads to a peaceful solution, rather than to continued fighting. Arguably, that is the best basis for defending "one person, one vote" as a rule of democracy against claims that those who have more

education, or who pay more taxes, or who have served in the military, or who believe in the one true God, or who are worse off should have additional votes because of their particular attributes.[32]

3. In practice, utilitarians can often support the principle of distributing resources to those who are worst off, because when you already have a lot, giving you more does not increase your utility as much as when you have only a little. One of the 1.2 billion people in the world living on $1 per day will get much more utility out of an additional $100 than will someone living on $60,000 per year. Similarly, if we have to take $100 from someone, we will cause much less suffering if we take it from the person earning $60,000 than if we take it from the person earning $365 a year. This is known as "diminishing marginal utility." When compared with giving resources to meet someone's core needs, giving further resources "at the margin" to someone else whose core needs have already been satisfied will lead to diminished utility. Hence a utilitarian will generally favor the worst-off when it comes to distributing resources. In contrast to Rawls, however, a utilitarian does not consider this principle to be absolute. The utilitarian always seeks the greatest overall benefit, and it is only a broad rule of thumb that this will generally be obtained by adding to the stock of resources of those who have the least.

The utilitarian would also have to take into account the greater hardship that might be imposed on people living in countries that have difficulty in complying with strict emission standards because their geography or climate compels their citizens to use a greater amount of energy to achieve a given level of comfort than do people living elsewhere. Canadians, for example, could argue that it would simply not be possible to live in many parts of their country without using above average quantities of energy to keep warm. Residents of rich countries might even advance the bolder claim that, since their affluent residents have become used to traveling by car, and keeping their houses cool in warm humid weather, they would suffer more if they have to give up their energy-intensive lifestyle than poorer people will suffer if they never get the chance to experience such comforts.

The utilitarian cannot refuse to consider such claims of hardship, even when they come from those who are already far better off than most of the world's people. As we shall see, however, these claims can be taken into account in a way that is compatible with the general conclusion to which the utilitarian view would otherwise lead: that the United States and other rich nations should bear much more of the burden of reducing greenhouse gas emissions than the poor nations—perhaps even the entire burden.

Fairness: A Proposal

Each of the four principles of fairness I have considered could be defended as the best one to take, or we could take some in combination. I propose, both because of its simplicity, and hence its suitability as a political compromise, and because it seems likely to increase global welfare, that we support the second principle, that of equal per capita future entitlements to a share of the capacity of the atmospheric sink, tied to the current United Nations projection of population growth per country in 2050.

Some will say that this is excessively harsh on industrialized nations like the United States, which will have to cut back the most on their output of greenhouse gases. But we have now seen that the equal per capita shares principle is much more indulgent to the United States and other developed nations than other principles for which there are strong arguments. If, for example, we combined "the polluter pays" principle with the equal share principle, we would hold that until the excessive amounts of greenhouse gases in the atmosphere that the industrialized nations have put there have been soaked up, the emissions of industrialized nations ought to be held down to much *less* than a per capita equal share. As things stand now, even on an equal per capita share basis, for at least a century the developing nations are going to have to accept lower outputs of greenhouse gases than they would have had to, if the industrialized nations had kept to an equal per capita share in the past. So by saying, "forget about the past, let's start anew," the pure equal per capita share principle is a lot more favorable to the developed countries than an historically based principle would be.

The fact that 178 nations, including every major industrial nation in the world except the United States, have now indicated their intention to ratify the Kyoto Protocol makes the position of the United States particularly odious from an ethical perspective. The claim that the Protocol does not require the developing nations to do their share does not stand up to scrutiny. Americans who think that even the Kyoto Protocol requires America to sacrifice more than it should are really demanding that the poor nations of the world commit themselves to a level that gives them, in perpetuity, lower levels of greenhouse gas production per head of population than the rich nations have. How could that principle be justified? Alternatively, if that is not what the U.S. Government is proposing, what exactly is it proposing?

It is true that there are some circumstances in which we are justified in refusing to contribute if others are not doing their share. If we eat communally and take turns cooking, then I can justifiably feel resentment if there are some who eat but never cook or carry out equivalent tasks for the good of the entire group. But that is not the situation with climate change, in which the behavior of the industrialized nations has been more like that of a person who has left the kitchen tap running but refuses either to turn it off, or to mop up the resulting flood, until you—who spilt an insignificant half-glass of water onto the floor—promise not to spill any more water. Now the other industrialized nations have agreed to turn off the tap (to be strictly accurate, to restrict the flow), leaving the United States, the biggest culprit, alone in its refusal to commit itself to reducing emissions.

Although it is true that the Kyoto Protocol does not initially bind the developing nations, it is generally understood that the developing countries will be brought into the binding section of the agreement after the industrialized nations have begun to move toward their targets. That was the procedure with the successful Montreal Protocol concerning gases that damage the ozone layer, and there is no reason to believe that it will not also happen with the Kyoto Protocol. China, by far the largest greenhouse gas emitter of the developing nations and the only one with the potential to rival the total—not, of course, per capita—emissions of the United States in the foreseeable future, has already, even in the absence of any binding targets, achieved a substantial decline in fossil-fuel CO_2 emissions, thanks to improved efficiency in coal use. Emissions fell from a high of 909 million metric tons of carbon in 1996 to 848 million metric tons of carbon in 1998. Meanwhile U.S. emissions reached an all-time high of 1,906 million metric tons of carbon in 2000, an increase of 2.5 percent over the previous year.[33]

The real objection to allocating the atmosphere's capacity to absorb greenhouse gases to nations on the basis of equal per capita shares is that it would be tremendously dislocating for the industrialized nations to reduce their emissions so much that, within 5, 10, or 15 years, they were not producing more than their share, on a per capita basis, of some acceptable level of greenhouse gases. But fortunately there is a mechanism that, while fully compatible with the equal per capita share principle, can make this transition much easier for the industrialized nations, while at the same time producing great benefits for the developing nations. That mechanism is emissions trading. Emissions trading works on the same simple economic principle of trade in general: if you can buy something from someone else more cheaply than you can produce it yourself, you are better off buying it than making it. In this case, what you can buy will be a transferable quota to produce greenhouse gases, allocated on the basis of an equal per capita share. A country like the United States that is already producing more gases than its share will need its full quota, and then some, but a country like Russia that is below its share will have excess quota that it can sell. If the quota were not transferable, the United States would immediately have to reduce its output to about 20 percent of what it now produces, a political impossibility. In contrast, Russia would have no incentive to maintain its levels of greenhouse gas emissions well below its allowable share. With emissions trading, Russia has an incentive to maximize the amount of quota it can sell, and the United States has, at some cost, an opportunity to acquire the quotas it needs to avoid total disruption of the economy.[34]

Although some may think that emissions trading allows the United States to avoid its burdens too easily, the point is not to punish nations with high emissions, but to produce the best outcome for the atmosphere. Permitting emissions trading gives us a better hope of doing this than prohibiting emissions trading does. The Kyoto Protocol as agreed to in Bonn and Marrakech allows emissions trading between states that have binding quotas. Thus Russia will have quota to sell, but countries like India, Bangladesh, Mozambique, Ethiopia, and many others will not. Emissions trading would be much more effective, and have far better consequences, if all nations were given binding quotas based on their per capita share of the designated total emissions. As we saw earlier in this chapter, even the environmental skeptic

Bjorn Lomborg accepts that with global emissions trading, the Kyoto Protocol produces a net economic benefit. Moreover, global emissions trading would give the world's poorest nations something that the rich nations very much want. They would have, at last, something that they can trade in exchange for the resources that will help them to meet their needs. This would be, on most principles of justice or utility, a very good thing indeed. It could also end the argument about making the developing nations part of a binding agreement on emissions, because the developing nations would see that they have a great deal to gain from binding quotas.

Since global emissions trading is both possible and desirable, it also answers two objections to allocating greenhouse gas emissions quotas on the basis of equal per capita shares. First, it answers the objection raised when discussing a utilitarian approach to these problems, that countries like Canada might suffer undue hardship if forced to limit emissions to the same per capita amount as, say, Mexico, because Canadians need to use more energy to survive their winters. But global emissions trading means that Canada would be able to buy the quota it requires from other countries that do not need their full quota. Thus the market would provide a measure of the additional burden put on the world's atmosphere by keeping one's house at a pleasant temperature when it is too cold, or too hot, outside. Citizens of rich countries could choose to pay that price and keep themselves warm, or cool, as the case may be. They would not, however, be claiming a benefit for themselves that they were not prepared to allow poor countries to have, because the poor countries would benefit by having emission quotas to sell. The claim of undue hardship therefore does not justify allowing rich countries to have a higher per capita emissions quota than poor countries.

Second, global emissions trading answers the objection that

equal per capita shares would lead to inefficient production because countries with little industrialization would be able to continue to manufacture goods even though they emit more greenhouse gases per unit of economic activity than highly industrialized nations, while the highly industrialized nations would have to cut back on their manufacturing capacity, even though they produce fewer emissions per unit of economic activity. But as we have seen, the present laissez-faire system allows emitters to reap economic benefits for themselves, while imposing costs on third parties who may or may not share in the benefits of the polluters' high productivity. That is neither a fair nor an efficient outcome. A well-regulated system of per capita entitlements combined with global emissions trading would, by internalizing the true costs of production, lead to a solution that is both fair and efficient.

There are two serious objections, one scientific and one ethical, to global emissions trading. The scientific objection is that we do not have the means to measure emissions accurately for all countries. Hence it would not be possible to know how much quota these countries have to sell, or need to buy. This is something that needs more research, but it should not prove an insuperable obstacle in the long run. As long as estimates are fair, they do not need to be accurate to the last ton of carbon. The ethical objection is that while emissions trading would benefit poor countries if the governments of those countries used it for the benefit of their people, some countries are run by corrupt dictators more interested in increasing their military spending, or adding to their Swiss bank accounts. Emissions trading would simply give them a new way of raising money for these purposes.

The ethical objection is similar to a problem discussed in the final section of the next chapter on trade, legitimacy, and democracy, and my proposed solution may be clearer after reading that section. It is to refuse to recognize a corrupt dictatorial regime, interested only in self-preservation and self-enrichment, as the legitimate government of the country that has excess quota to sell. In the absence of any legitimate government that can receive payments for quota, the sale of quota could be managed by an international authority answerable to the United Nations. That authority could hold the money it receives in trust until the country has a government able to make a credible claim that the money will be used to benefit the people as a whole.

Down from the Clouds?

To cynical observers of the Washington scene, all this must seem absurdly lacking in political realism. George W. Bush's administration has spurned the Kyoto Protocol, which allows the United States to continue to produce at least four times its per capita share of carbon dioxide. Since 1990 U.S. emission levels have already risen by 14 percent. The half-hearted measures for energy conservation proposed by the Bush administration will, at best, slow that trend. They will not reverse it. So what is the point of discussing proposals that are far *less* likely to be accepted by the U.S. Government than the Kyoto Protocol?

The aim of this chapter is to help us to see that there is no *ethical* basis for the present distribution of the atmosphere's capacity to absorb greenhouse gases without drastic climate change. If the industrialized countries choose to retain this distribution (as the United States does), or to use it as the starting point for a new allocation of the capacity of the global sink (as the countries that accept the Kyoto Protocol do), they are standing simply on their presumed rights as sovereign nations. That claim, and the raw military power these nations yield, makes it impossible for anyone else to impose a more ethically defensible solution on them. If we, as citizens of the industrialized nations, do not understand what would be a fair solution to global warming, then we cannot understand how flagrantly self-serving the position of those opposed to signing even the Kyoto Protocol is. If, on the other hand, we can convey to our fellow citizens a sense of what would be a fair solution to the problem, then it may be possible to change the policies that are now leading the United States to block international cooperation on something that will have an impact on every being on this planet.

Let us consider the implications of this situation a little further. Today the overwhelming majority of nations in the world are united in the view that greenhouse gas emissions should be significantly reduced, and all the major industrial nations but one have committed themselves to doing something about this. That one nation, which happens to be the largest emitter of them all, has refused to commit itself to reducing its emissions. Such a situation gives impetus to the need to think about developing institutions or principles of international law that limit national sovereignty. It should be possible for people whose lands are flooded by sea level rises due to global warming to win damages from nations that emit more than their fair share of greenhouse gases. Another possibility worth considering is sanctions. There have been several occasions on which the United Nations has used sanctions against countries that have been seen as doing something gravely wrong. Arguably the case for sanctions against a nation that is causing harm, often fatal, to the citizens of other countries is even stronger than the case for sanctions against a country like South Africa under apartheid, since that government, iniquitous as its policies were, was not a threat to other countries. (Though whether that is any defense against intervention for a regime that violates the rights of its own citizens is the topic of Chapter 4.) Is it inconceivable that one day a reformed and strengthened United Nations will invoke sanctions against countries that do not play their part in global measures for the protection of the environment?

3 one economy

The World Trade Organization Fracas

If there is one organization that critics of globalization point to as responsible for pushing the process onward—and in the wrong way—it is the World Trade Organization. Tony Clarke, director of the Ottawa-based Polaris Institute, expresses a now-widespread view when he describes the WTO as the mechanism for "accelerating and extending the transfer of peoples' sovereignty from nation states to global corporations."[1] We have become so familiar with protests against the development of a single global economy that it is already difficult to recall the mentality of the period before the December 1999 Seattle meeting of the WTO, when the very existence of that organization had barely penetrated the minds of most Americans. Before the dramatic events in Seattle, if the popular media mentioned the WTO at all it was in glowing terms of the economic benefits that were flowing from the expansion of world trade. Since, as the most prevalent metaphor of the time put it, "a rising tide lifts all boats," these benefits were bound to reach the poorest nations as well. Very few people had any idea that there was serious opposition to the WTO and its program of removing barriers to world trade. Television footage from Seattle of demonstrators dressed as sea turtles protesting against WTO decisions, anarchists in black tights throwing bricks at the commanding heights of global capitalism, and ordinary American unionists marching against cheap imports made by child labor awakened the American public to the existence of opposition to the WTO. When the protesters unexpectedly proved capable of disrupting the schedules of presidents and prime ministers, they immediately became front-page news. Their impact was reinforced when the new round of trade negotiations expected to begin in Seattle failed to get started. Even then, the initial response of media commentators was bewilderment, incomprehension, and ridicule. Thomas Friedman wrote an intemperate op-ed piece for the *New York Times* that began by asking: "Is there anything more ridiculous in the news today than the protests against the World Trade Organization in Seattle?" He went on to call the protestors "a Noah's ark of flat-earth advocates, protectionist trade unions and yuppies looking for their 1960's fix."[2] These "ridiculous" protestors succeeded in generating a whole new debate about the impact of world trade and the WTO.

Has any non-criminal organization ever been so vehemently condemned on such wide-ranging grounds by critics from so many different countries as the WTO? According to Victor Menotti, director of the Environment Program of the U.S.-based International Forum on Globalization, the regime of trade and investment fostered by the WTO has "unleashed global economic forces that systematically punish ecologically sound forestry while rewarding destructive practices that accelerate forest degradation."[3] From the standpoint of Compassion in World Farming, a leading British campaigner for farm animals, the WTO is "The Biggest Threat Facing Animal Welfare Today."[4] Martin Khor, the Malaysia-based leader of the Third World Network, claims that the WTO is "an instrument to govern the South."[5] Vandana Shiva, founder and president of India's Research Foundation for Science, Technology and Ecology and author of *Biopiracy: The Plunder of Nature and Knowledge,* writes that the rules of the WTO are "primarily rules of robbery, camouflaged by arithmetic and legalese," and global free trade in food and agriculture is "the biggest refugee creation program in the world." It is, not to put too fine a point on it, "leading to slavery."[6] All in all, many of these critics would agree with the summary judgment attributed to the Zapatistas, an organization of Mexican peasants, that the WTO is simply "the biggest enemy of mankind."[7]

A few weeks after the failure of the Seattle meeting, I found myself in Davos, Switzerland, as an invited speaker at the annual meeting of the World Economic Forum. Pre-Seattle attitudes—and a baffled incomprehension about the protests—were still evident. I heard politicians like President Ernesto Zedillo of Mexico, and corporate leaders like Lewis Campbell, chief executive of Textron, a corporation with a turnover of $10 billion a year, swiftly dismiss the protesters as falling into one of two groups: those who were well-intentioned in their concern to protect the environment or help the world's poorest people but were naïve and misled by their emotions; and those who, under the cynical guise of defending human rights and the environment, were seeking to protect their own well-paid jobs in inefficient industries by high tariff barriers that raise costs for domestic consumers and leave workers in less developed countries stuck in dire poverty.

There were dissenting voices at Davos—U.S. labor leader

John Sweeney and Martin Khor spoke against the dominant view, but at first they found little resonance among the large international audience of corporate chieftains and heads of government departments of economics and finance. Then British Prime Minister Tony Blair and U.S. President Bill Clinton showed that they were quicker learners than most of the corporate chief executives present, saying that genuine issues had been raised and they needed serious consideration. Nevertheless there was no real discussion of what those issues might be or of how they might be resolved. It was as if everyone already knew that globalization was economically beneficial, and "good for the economy" was identical in meaning to "good all things considered." So the real question was how to brush off the vexing opposition and make faster headway toward the goal of a single world economy, free of all barriers to trade or investment between different states. The alternative was, in Zedillo's word, just "globaphobia."[8]

The International Forum on Globalization helped to organize the protests at Seattle and is one of the WTO's most prominent critics. In September 2000, to coincide with the Millennium Assembly of the United Nations, the IFG held a forum on "Globalization and the Role of the United Nations," in New York. It was a sharp contrast to the Davos meeting. For ten hours speaker after speaker blasted the WTO and global corporate power. No one supportive of the WTO had been invited to speak, and there was no opportunity to ask questions or discuss anything that had been said. Though the IFG advocates grassroots involvement in decision-making, the World Economic Forum allowed more audience participation and presented a greater diversity of viewpoints.

As the protests at meetings of the WTO, the World Bank and other international bodies continue—from Seattle to Washington D.C., Prague, Melbourne, Quebec City, Gothenburg, Genoa, and New York—genuine open-minded exploration of the crucial and difficult issues arising from globalization is losing out to partisan polemics, long in rhetoric and thin in substance, with each side speaking only to its own supporters who already know who the saints and sinners are. Endlessly repeated rituals of street theater do not provide opportunities for the kind of discussion that is needed. Economics raises questions of value, and economists tend to be too focused on markets to give sufficient importance to values that are not dealt with well by the market.

The Four Charges

Among the many charges commonly made against the WTO, four are central to any assessment of the role that the WTO, and economic globalization more generally, plays in forming a world that is different from anything that has existed up to now:

1. The WTO places economic considerations ahead of concerns for the environment, animal welfare, and even human rights.
2. The WTO erodes national sovereignty.
3. The WTO is undemocratic.
4. The WTO increases inequality; or (a stronger charge) it makes the rich richer and leaves the world's poorest people even worse off than they would otherwise have been.

Before we can consider these charges, we need some background. The World Trade Organization was created by the "Uruguay Round" of talks held by member nations of the General Agreement on Tariffs and Trade, or GATT. It came into existence in January 1995, and by January 2002 had 144 member nations, accounting for more than 97 percent of world trade.[9] Although it seems as if the WTO is a new organization, it is essentially the successor to GATT, which has been around for fifty years. Its raison d'être is also the same as that of GATT, namely the belief that free trade makes people better off, on average and in the long run. This belief is based on the usual rationale of the market, that if two people have different abilities to make products that they both desire, they will do better if they each work in the areas of production where they are most efficient (or least inefficient) relative to the other person, and then exchange, rather than if they both try to make the full range of products they want. This will be true, it is claimed, whether the people are neighbors or live on opposite sides of the world, as long as the transaction costs involved in making the exchange are less than the differences in their costs of production. Moreover this exchange should be particularly good for countries with low labor costs, because they should be able to produce goods more cheaply than countries with high labor costs. Hence we can expect the demand for labor in those countries to rise, and once the supply of labor begins to tighten, wages should rise too. Thus a free market should have the effect not only of making the world as a whole more prosperous, but more specifically, of assisting the poorest nations.

The agreement by which the WTO was set up gives it the power to enforce a set of rules and agreements relating to free trade that now total about 30,000 pages.[10] If one member nation believes that it is disadvantaged by actions taken by another member nation that are in breach of these rules, the first nation can make a complaint. If efforts to mediate the dispute fail, a dispute panel, consisting of experts in trade and law, is set up to hear it. These dispute panels are the most distinctive difference between the old GATT and the new WTO. In formal terms, the dispute panel does not decide the dispute but recommends a decision to the membership. In practice the decision of the dispute panel is invariably adopted. If the complaint is upheld and the member nation continues to act in breach of WTO rules, it can be subjected to severe penalties, including tariffs against its own goods.

We can now consider in turn the four charges against the WTO.

The First Charge: Economics as Trumps

At first glance it is not obvious why an organization concerned with removing barriers to trade should interfere with protection of the environment, animal welfare, or human rights. Indeed, the WTO claims that this perception is all a misunderstanding. In a publication called *10 Common Misunderstandings about the WTO,* clearly aimed at a broad audience, the fourth in the list of ten "misunderstandings" discussed is:

> In the WTO, commercial interests take precedence over environmental protection.

In explaining why this is a misunderstanding, the publication points out that the WTO dispute panel report on the sea turtle case explicitly stated that members of the WTO "can, should and do take measures to protect endangered species." The publication then adds:

> What's important in the WTO's rules is that measures taken to protect the environment must not be unfair. For example, they must not discriminate. You cannot be lenient with your own producers and at the same time be strict with foreign goods and services.[11]

That sounds like a very reasonable principle. The WTO allows member nations to protect endangered species as long as they do so fairly and do not, under the guise of environmental protection, favor their own industries. Presumably, then, the United States could, for example, prohibit the import of tuna caught by methods that drown dolphins, as long as it also prohibits the sale of tuna caught by American ships in American waters that catch tuna by this method. If this presumption is correct, then the critics of the WTO seem wrong in their allegations that the organization is opposed to measures to protect the environment. The WTO opposes, it seems, only measures that use environmental protection as a guise for the protection of domestic industries against foreign competition. If the WTO struck down U.S. laws to protect dolphin or sea turtles for those reasons, the fault must lie with the United States for drafting laws that favor its own producers, rather than with the WTO.

The meeting of ministers from WTO governments in Doha (capital of Qatar, on the Persian Gulf) in November 2001 agreed to a Ministerial Declaration that endorsed the same principle:

> We recognize that under WTO rules no country should be prevented from taking measures for the protection of human, animal or plant life or health, or of the environment at the levels it considers appropriate, subject to the requirement that they are not applied in a manner which would constitute a means of arbitrary or unjustifiable discrimination between countries where the same conditions prevail, or a disguised restriction on international trade, and are otherwise in accordance with the provisions of the WTO Agreements.[12]

This is not, however, how the WTO dispute panels have reached their decisions up to now, and if this clause in the Ministerial Declaration really becomes effective, it will be a dramatic break with the past. Consider, for example, the "Tuna-Dolphin Dispute," which although decided under GATT rather than the WTO, still sets out principles that the WTO uses. Here is an account of the dispute given in the WTO publication *Trading into the Future* (which provides a rather less simplistic account of how the WTO works than *10 Common Misunderstandings*):

> The U.S. Marine Mammal Protection Act sets dolphin protection standards for the domestic American fishing fleet and for countries whose fishing boats catch yellowfin tuna in that part of the Pacific Ocean [where schools of dolphin swim over schools of tuna]. If a country exporting tuna to the United States cannot prove to the U.S. authorities that it meets the dolphin protection standards set out in U.S. law, the U.S. government must embargo all imports of fish from that country. In this case Mexico was the exporting country concerned. Its exports of yellowfin tuna to the U.S. were banned.[13]

In other words, the U.S. Marine Mammal Protection Act was not lenient toward U.S. domestic producers while being strict to foreign producers. It applied the same standards to everyone. In effect, Congress had said: "We think it wrong to trap and drown dolphins unnecessarily while catching tuna, and we are not going to allow any tuna caught in that way to be sold in the U.S." So if the WTO were to exclude environmental protection laws only when they favor one's own country, presumably when Mexico complained to GATT about the U.S. embargo, its complaint would have been thrown out? But the GATT panel concluded, as *Trading into the Future* notes:

> that the U.S. could not embargo imports of tuna products from Mexico simply because Mexican regulations on *the way the tuna was produced* did not satisfy U.S. regulations. (But the U.S. could apply its regulations on *the quality or content* of the tuna imported.) This has become known as a "product" versus "process" issue.[14]

The Misuse of the Product/Process Distinction

This "product" versus "process" distinction is crucial to understanding the impact of WTO rules in many areas. As the tuna-
dolphin case exemplifies, and as later decisions have reiterated,
the WTO operates on the basis that a country cannot ban a product on the basis of the process by which the product was made
but only by showing that the banned product is different in its
inherent nature from other products. In matters relating to the
killing or mistreatment of animals alone, for example, apart from
the tuna-dolphin case, the WTO has had the following impact:

- In 1991 the European Union agreed to prohibit, from 1995, the
  sale of furs that had come from animals caught in steel-jaw
  leghold traps. (These traps crush and hold the animal's leg,
  holding the animal until the trapper returns, which may be
  several days. Nocturnal animals are terrified at being held out
  in daylight. Animals may die of thirst or from their injuries.
  They have been known to bite off their own legs to get free.)
  Because it is impossible to tell if an individual pelt has come
  from an animal caught in one of these traps, or by some
  relatively more humane method, the European Union decided
  to accept the import of furs only from countries that had
  banned the steel-jaw leghold trap. The United States, Canada,
  and Russia threatened to lodge a complaint with the WTO
  against this ban. The European Union capitulated, allowing
  fur caught with steel-jaw leghold traps to continue to be sold in
  Europe.[15]
- In 1993 the European Union adopted a directive preventing the
  use of animals in cosmetics testing and prohibiting, by 1998,
  the sale of cosmetics that had been tested on animals. But the
  European Union was advised that the prohibition on the sale

of cosmetics tested on animals would be a breach of WTO rules. The ban was never implemented.[16]

• In 1989, after prolonged public campaigning, the European Union banned the sale of beef from cattle treated with growth-promoting hormones. Health concerns were the main reason given for the ban, although animal welfare organizations have expressed concern about the implications of the hormones for the health of the cattle.[17] The United States successfully challenged the ban at the WTO, with the WTO panel finding that there was not sufficient scientific basis for believing that the use of the hormones posed a risk to human health. The European Union appealed, but the WTO's appellate body also found in favor of the United States. When the European Union nevertheless refused to lift the ban, the WTO authorized the United States to retaliate by imposing 100 percent duties on $116 million of EU agricultural products.[18]

The decisions in all of these cases rest on the claim that the product—the fur, the cosmetic, the beef—is the same *product* as other products allowed to be sold in the country, and the fact that they are the outcome of a different *process* is irrelevant. But why is it irrelevant? What does the product/process distinction have to do with the rejection of unfair trading practices that, according to *10 Common Misunderstandings,* is the reason why the WTO prohibits some forms of environmental protection? At first glance, nothing at all. But *Trading into the Future* suggests the following link:

> What was the reason behind . . . [the tuna-dolphin] ruling? If the U.S. arguments were accepted, then any country could ban imports of a product from another country merely because the exporting country has different

environmental, health and social policies from its own.
This would create a virtually open-ended route for any
country to apply trade restrictions unilaterally . . . the door
would be opened to a possible flood of protectionist
abuses.[19]

Now we can see how misleading the statement in *10 Common
Misunderstandings* is. In that document the WTO defends itself
by claiming that under its rules, environmental protection measures are prohibited only if those measures treat foreign producers more harshly than domestic producers. But what really happens when the WTO considers a case where the law is applied
fairly to both domestic and foreign producers? The issue becomes, not whether foreign producers were in fact treated more
harshly than domestic producers, but whether allowing a country
to prohibit a product because of the way in which it was produced could open the door to "a flood of protectionist abuses."
Even if we assume that this flood really would occur, the argument assumes that the value of preventing such a flood of protectionist abuses is greater than the value of protecting the environment, animals, and community peace of mind—greater, for
example, than the value of protecting millions of dolphins from
cruel and premature death, of stopping the barbarity of the steel-
jaw leghold trap, or of providing the public with the peace of
mind they seek in respect to their concerns about the hazards of
hormone-treated beef. And these are just three among the count-
less things we value that our governments might, but for WTO
rulings, see fit to protect by prohibiting the import of products
produced in ways we consider objectionable. Import prohibitions against goods produced in ways that violate human rights
—for example, by using forced labor, or pushing indigenous
people off their land—would also fail to pass the test of being ap-

plied to a product, rather than a process. If any form of protection, no matter how fair it is in the way it treats domestic and foreign enterprises, is ruled out because it targets a process rather than a product, that will drastically curtail the means by which a nation can protect its values.

In any case, there is no solid ground for believing that the product/process distinction is the only way to stop a flood of protectionist legislation. There are more finely grained ways in which dispute panels—made up of, the WTO tells us, experts in trade and law—can distinguish disguised or unjustifiable protectionism from reasonable measures to protect the environment. The first test should be, as both *10 Common Misunderstandings* and the November 2001 WTO Ministerial Declaration suggest, whether the measure taken to protect the environment or animal welfare, or whatever other legitimate objectives a nation may have, deals evenhandedly with the nation's own producers and with foreign producers. If it does, then the measure is prima facie acceptable, and any nation seeking to have it invalidated should be required to show that the environmental or other objectives the measure purports to aim at could reasonably have been achieved without restricting trade to the extent that the measure does restrict it.

Trading into the Future claims, in the passage just quoted, that if the U.S. argument in the tuna-dolphin case had been accepted, "any country could ban imports of a product from another country merely because the exporting country has different environmental, health and social policies from its own." The use of the term "merely" here is noteworthy, for the "different policies" in the exporting countries might be ones permitting the dumping of toxic wastes into the ocean, extreme cruelty to animals, or denying workers the right to unionize. The implication is that these are somehow less important reasons for banning a product than those that are concerned with the inherent qualities of a product, which the WTO would unhesitatingly accept, as long as the bans did not discriminate between domestic and foreign producers. There is, however, no reason to think that our support for the environment, for animals, and for human rights is any less important than the desire to protect one's citizens from products that are of inferior quality.

In any case, the suggestion that the importing country is, by banning the product made in ways harmful to the environment or to animals or to workers, trying to exercise extraterritorial powers over the exporting country is misleading. This may be the case, and it would not necessarily be wrong—as we shall see in the next chapter, it is sometimes justifiable to intervene militarily to prevent flagrant human rights abuses in other countries, so it can hardly always be wrong to try to prevent such abuses by trade measures—but it is not true that any prohibition of a product made in another country because of the process by which that product is made *must* be an attempt to exercise extraterritorial powers. Just as a country might ban the sale of a pesticide, whether of domestic or foreign origin, because it is toxic to wildlife—and to that ban the WTO would not object—so a country might ban the sale of a product, whether domestic or foreign, because the process by which it is made is toxic to wildlife. Wild animals need not be seen as the property of one country. The process by which the product is made might kill migratory birds or, as with the dolphin and sea turtle cases, animals living in the oceans. Even when the animals killed live entirely within the borders of the country making the product, however, the country seeking to ban the product may think that it is wrong to be indifferent to the death and suffering of animals and may find it morally objectionable for a product made in a way that displays such indifference to be sold within its jurisdiction. The ethical argument that motivates the other chapters of this book is relevant here too: just as there is no sound reason why the citizens of a state should be concerned solely with the interests of their fellow citizens, rather than with the interests of people everywhere, so there is no sound reason why the citizens of a state should be concerned with the well-being of animals only when those animals are living within the boundaries of their own state. Given this, if a state decides that the steel-jaw leghold trap is cruel and immoral, and it prohibits within its own borders the use of the trap as well as the sale of any furs that come from animals trapped in that manner, this decision comes squarely within the conventionally accepted powers of sovereignty over its own territory. If this principle of preventing the sale of morally objectionable products within one's own borders is rejected, then how could a country be justified in prohibiting the import of films that display acts of real, non-consensual sexual violence, even sexual violence resulting in death (as in so-called "snuff movies")? No one regards prohibiting such films as objectionable because it is an attempt by one nation to prevent the "extraterritorial" rape and murder of women and children. Yet here too it is the "process" that is the reason for the prohibition. The final product may be indistinguishable from a film in which skilled actors who are not harmed perform the same scenes. As far as claims of "extraterritoriality" are concerned, it is hard to discern a difference of principle between the prohibition of snuff movies and the prohibition of furs from leghold traps.

It would, of course, be both possible and consistent with the overall argument of this book to favor a reduction in the significance of national sovereignty and to hold that global or transnational bodies should decide such issues. But that cannot happen until there are such bodies, with procedures—hopefully democratic and responsive to public opinion—by which these questions can be decided.

The Undermining of GATT's Article XX

Notwithstanding the use that the WTO disputes panels have made of the product/process distinction, one article of the General Agreement on Tariffs and Trade appears to give explicit blessing to import bans undertaken for various purposes, including the protection of the environment. Article XX reads, in its relevant sections, as follows:

> General Exceptions
> Subject to the requirement that such measures are not applied in a manner which would constitute a means of arbitrary or unjustifiable discrimination between countries where the same conditions prevail, or a disguised restriction on international trade, nothing in this Agreement shall be construed to prevent the adoption or enforcement by any contracting party of measures:
> (a) necessary to protect public morals;
> (b) necessary to protect human, animal or plant life or health; . . .
> (g) relating to the conservation of exhaustible natural resources if such measures are made effective in conjunction with restrictions on domestic production or consumption.

The most natural reading of this article would give a country several grounds on which it could prohibit the importation of goods obtained in ways that threaten dolphins or cause great suffering to animals. Clause (b) allows exceptions to protect animal life, and clause (g) allows an exception to conserve "exhaustible natural resources." A prohibition on importing products produced by unethical methods of fishing or by the use of cruel traps could also be justified by clause (a), which refers to the protection of "public morals." If this means the morals people actually have, then there are many countries in which the unnecessary killing of animals, especially those of endangered species, offends against moral standards widely held by the general public. The sale of products that result from such killing is as offensive to public morals as, say nudity would be in some countries. If, on the other hand, the clause referring to the protection of public morals is intended to refer to sound moral values, irrespective of how widely they are held, then the case against products obtained by cruel methods is much *stronger* than the case against mere nudity.

In the sea turtle case the United States argued that its prohibition on the importation of shrimp caught by fishing fleets not using devices to exclude sea turtles was allowable under clauses (b) and (g) of Article XX. After this argument was rejected by the dispute panel on grounds consistent with the tuna/dolphin case, the U.S. appealed, but the appeal was again rejected. This time the WTO's Appellate Body did accept that a measure to protect endangered species could fall under the exemptions. It nevertheless rejected the U.S. shrimp prohibition on the grounds that it required essentially the same methods of excluding turtles used by domestic vessels to be used by other nations, instead of allowing other methods of avoiding the killing of turtles. As the Appellate Body put it:

> We believe that discrimination results not only when countries in which the same conditions prevail are differently treated, but also when the application of the measure at issue does not allow for any inquiry into the appropriateness of the regulatory program for the conditions prevailing in those exporting countries.[20]

At one point in its judgment the Appellate Body remarked that "it is relevant to observe that an import prohibition is, ordinarily, the heaviest 'weapon' in a Member's armoury of trade measures" (par. 171), an observation that apparently leads it to take the view that all other avenues for achieving the desired objective must have been exhausted before an import prohibition can be adopted. The United States then entered into negotiations with other countries to reach a multilateral agreement on the use of turtle-excluding devices. Meanwhile it retained its ban on the importation of shrimp caught by ships not using such devices. Again a dispute arose about the ban, and finally, in November 2001, the Appellate Body accepted that the United States was doing enough. As long as the United States was engaging in "ongoing, serious good faith efforts" to reach a multilateral agreement on the protection of sea turtles, the import ban could remain in place.[21]

Perhaps the decision in the sea turtle case—the only example in the entire history of both GATT and the WTO that a unilateral, extraterritorial national measure involving trade restrictions has been upheld on environmental grounds—is evidence that since Seattle the WTO has become more sensitive to criticism of its environmental record. Certainly, an examination of that record prior to November 2001 justifies the statement with which we began: "In the WTO, commercial interests take precedence over environmental protection." Far from being a misunderstanding, this has turned out to be true. Whenever a dispute has required a choice between free trade and support for a non-discriminatory national policy intended to protect the environment, the WTO's verdict before November 2001 was that the policy is an illegal barrier to trade.[22] The WTO justified these decisions either on the basis of the product/process distinction or because the restriction is supposedly arbitrary or unjustifiable discrimination. There are two possible justifications for the product/process rule. The first is the claim that to prohibit a product because of the way in which it is made is to attempt to exercise extraterritorial jurisdiction. We have seen that this argument is spurious. The second possible justification is that to depart from the product/process rule may make it more difficult to distinguish genuine measures for protecting the environment, or other legitimate concerns, from disguised forms of protectionism. Regarding that justification as sufficient to reject the environmental protection policy does give commercial interests precedence over environmental protection. Where the Appellate Body has found arbitrary or unjustifiable discrimination, it has been able to reach this finding only because it requires that the trade restriction be the last possible resort after every other avenue has been exhausted. Like the product/process rule, this criterion means that, whatever the Appellate Body may say, the substance of its decisions shows clearly that "commercial interests take precedence over environmental protection." In fairness, it needs to be said that these commercial interests may be those of the developing nations, as well as those of the developed nations. Either way, the record of the WTO to date enables us to see why Leestcffy Jenkins and Robert Stumberg, experts in law and animal protection reviewing that record for the Humane Society of the United States, should claim that, "in effect, free-market theory preempts all other social values."[23]

November 2001 *may* prove to be a watershed month for the WTO, because in addition to the ground-breaking decision in the sea turtle case, that month also saw signs, at the WTO Ministerial meeting in Doha, of a willingness to reconsider the rules ensuring that free trade trumps other values. As we have already seen, the Ministerial Declaration contained language suggesting that WTO rules should not prevent member nations from protecting the environment and animal and plant health, as long as they do so evenhandly. In addition, at the insistence of the European Union, the meeting allowed for the inclusion of, in the next round of trade talks, discussions on "non-trade concerns" in agriculture. One of these concerns is maintaining the economy of rural areas where the local economy depends on small farms that would not be able to withstand competition from other countries where farming is on a much larger scale. Preserving village life and the traditional European landscape is a value that needs to be considered alongside the benefits of free trade. Another legitimate concern is animal welfare. The European Union, which has relatively enlightened legislation on the treatment of farm animals, is seeking to ensure that its farmers will not have to face competition from other countries that permit forms of cruelty to animals not allowed in Europe. The Ministerial Declaration noted these concerns and agreed that they would be part of the negotiations on the next round of measures to liberalize trade, to be concluded by 2005.[24]

It remains to be seen whether, in the negotiations to come, values other than that of free trade will be given real weight. If they are not, we will all know that, in signing the 2001 Doha Ministerial Declaration (with its plain statement that evenhandedness and non-discrimination are the only requirements that the WTO imposes on countries seeking to protect the environment), the delegations of the WTO's member nations were either themselves deceived about how the WTO really operates or were trying to deceive the rest of the world.

The Second Charge: Interference with National Sovereignty

If the WTO does give precedence to commercial interests, is it reasonable to say that it does so only at the behest of its member states, which have the final decision on whether or not to go along with the WTO's rules? The standard response by WTO supporters to the claim that the organization overrides national sovereignty is that it is no more than the administrative framework for a set of agreements or treaties freely entered into by sovereign governments. Every member-nation of the WTO is a member because its government has decided to join, and has not subsequently decided to leave. Moreover decisions on matters other than the resolution of disputes are generally reached by consensus. Since the WTO is an expression of the decisions of sovereign governments, it is not something that can interfere with national sovereignty.

This account of the WTO as merely the administrator of a set of multilateral agreements may be true in formal terms, but it leaves out some important practical details. Once a government joins the WTO, it and its successors come under considerable pressure to remain a member. Export industries based on free trade develop, employing substantial numbers of people, and the threat that these industries will collapse if the nation withdraws from the treaties administered by the WTO becomes so potent that going one's own way becomes almost unthinkable. This is a form of Friedman's "Golden Straitjacket." In the WTO's eyes it is a good thing, because it means "good discipline" for governments, discourages "unwise" policies, and is good for business.[25] But it is not always true that what is good for business is good overall. A policy that the WTO considers "unwise" may have merits that do not count for much in its calculus of values.

While it is true that nations are free—at a price—to stay outside the WTO, or to leave it, when nations are members they can have their sovereignty significantly curtailed—and this is far from a trivial matter. The recent history of the availability of drugs for the treatment of AIDS in Africa indicates the crucial importance of getting these matters right. In South Africa alone, at the end of 2001, more than 4 million people—or 20 percent of the adult population—were infected with HIV, the virus that causes AIDS. In the rich nations, to have the virus is no longer a death sentence, because there are drugs that effectively, and as far as we know indefinitely, suppress the infection. But the drugs cost about $10,000 per person a year, far out of reach of almost all infected Africans. In this desperate situation, the South African government floated the idea of licensing manufacture of the drugs in South Africa, a procedure known as "compulsory licensing," and a recognized means of dealing with a health emergency. Local manufacture would mean that the drugs could be produced at a cost of about $350 a year. Even this sum is too much for many Africans, who live in countries in which the annual per capita spending on health care is about $10. But $350 a year is a realistic amount for some, especially South Africans.

When the South African government began to consider the possibility of licensing local drug manufacture, the United States responded with the threat of trade sanctions to defend the intellectual property rights of the drug manufacturers. After pressure from AIDS activists, the Clinton Administration dropped this threat. The world's major pharmaceutical corporations then went to court to stop South Africa from providing life-saving treatment for its people at a price that they could afford. In April 2001 public outrage led them to abandon their case and enter into arrangements to supply their products to African nations free or at greatly reduced prices. In October of the same year, amidst the bioterrorism panic that followed the discovery of anthrax in letters addressed to prominent Americans, the Canadian government announced that it would compulsorily license the manufacture of Cipro, the antibiotic most effective against anthrax. With some American politicians calling on the U.S. Government to follow Canada's lead, the U.S. Secretary for Health and Human Services instead persuaded Bayer, the pharmaceutical corporation that holds the patent for Cipro, to slash the drug's price. If they were not willing to do so, he made it clear, the United States would buy a cheaper generic version. Not surprisingly, since the U.S. Government was still trying to restrict the ways in which

African countries could obtain generic anti-AIDS drugs, the pressure that the U.S. Government put on Bayer led to an immediate outcry that the Administration was using one standard for protecting Americans—only a handful of whom had been infected with anthrax—and another for African countries, with an estimated 25 million people infected with the AIDS virus.[26]

Though the anthrax outbreak was a tragedy for the unlucky few who were its victims, its timing could not have been better for millions of people needing cheaper drugs, because it came just before the November 2001 Doha WTO Ministerial meeting. The developed nations, embarrassed by the accusation of double standards, agreed to a declaration that the WTO Agreement on Trade-Related Aspects of Intellectual Property Rights (known as the TRIPS Agreement) "does not and should not prevent Members from taking measures to protect public health." The declaration added that each Member "has the right to determine what constitutes a national emergency or other circumstances of extreme urgency" and specifically included "HIV/AIDS, tuberculosis, malaria and other epidemics" as representing such a situation, in which compulsory licensing of necessary drugs is permissible.[27]

Despite this highly encouraging development, the issue shows how sharply trade agreements can intrude into the most vital decisions a government can face. Granted, South Africa, as a free and sovereign nation, did not have to take part in the original TRIPS agreement. But there may have been substantial economic costs in refusing to take part. If nations, once they join the WTO, can lose significant national sovereignty in important areas, and if they are under constant pressure to remain in the WTO, the view that the WTO is no threat to national sovereignty is simplistic.

If we conclude that a nation under pressure to remain a member of the WTO has diminished national sovereignty, that is not in itself grounds for condemning the WTO. The loss of national sovereignty might be a price worth paying for the benefits the WTO brings. The choice is either to enter the agreement or not, and presumably those governments that decide to enter the agreement judge it to be better to do so, both for their own generation and for future generations. Before we criticize the WTO for eroding national sovereignty, then, we should ask: Is there any alternative means by which nations and their citizens could gain these benefits?

Traditionally those on the left, now ranged in opposition to the WTO, have been internationalists, whereas conservatives have been nationalists, opposing any constraints on state sovereignty. It is because the WTO puts free trade above both environmental values and national sovereignty that opposition to the WTO brings together such strange allies, from left and right. The alliance would split if the WTO were to be reformed in a way that enabled it to protect workers' rights and the environment, since this would give it more, rather than fewer, of the powers of global governance. Thus it would satisfy some critics on the left, but it would further inflame the nationalists on the right. The WTO's critics on the left support the supremacy of national legislatures and defend their right to make laws to protect the environment because they believe that the legislators are at least answerable to the people. Global corporations are not, and the WTO, in the eyes of the left, makes it too easy for global corporations to do as they please. This suggests that the WTO could meet the criticisms from the left—if not those from the right—by claiming that it provides the possibility of democratic rule over the global corporations. Then just as in the philosophy of social contract theorists like Rousseau, people forming a political community give up some of their individual freedom in order to gain a voice in the running of the whole community, so nations entering the WTO would give up some of their national sovereignty in order to gain a voice in the running of the global economy. This brings us to the third charge against the WTO.

The Third Charge: The WTO Is Undemocratic

That the WTO is undemocratic is another of the *10 Common Misunderstandings* that the organization would like to dispel. In rebuttal, the WTO publication asserts:

> Decisions in the WTO are generally by consensus. In principle, that's even more democratic than majority rule because everyone has to agree.

That is a very strange view of democracy. Rule by consensus can also be called rule by the veto—it takes the opposition of only a single member to stop an overwhelming majority from making changes. Since green groups are usually favorably inclined toward consensus decision-making, if the WTO really did offer a forum in which every member-nation has an equal chance to influence a decision by withholding its consent, this might be an effective ad hominem riposte to claims by the greens that the WTO is undemocratic. But the idea that giving everyone the right of veto is "even more democratic than majority rule" is false and given that at least one party is always likely to favor that with which they are familiar, or to benefit from the way things are currently done, this decision procedure is likely to help preserve the status quo.

There is another problem with the way in which the WTO makes decisions. Developing countries make up the majority of members of the WTO, but *10 Common Misunderstandings* concedes: "It would be wrong to suggest that every country has the same bargaining power." Indeed it would. In practice, the agenda is set by informal meetings of the major trading powers, especially, up to now, the United States, the European Union, Japan, and Canada. On major issues, once these powers have reached agreement, the results are presented to the formal meeting, but by then they often are a fait accompli.[28] Moreover, the poorer nations often lack the resources to participate fully in the innumerable WTO meetings. Some of them cannot even afford to maintain an office in Geneva, one of the world's most expensive cities, where the WTO has its headquarters. Others do have a mission in Geneva, but their staff must also cover the many United Nations agencies that are based there. In addition, while it is true that decisions in the WTO are generally taken by consensus, obviously dispute resolution decisions cannot be taken by consensus.

The WTO's publication also asserts, in defense of the democratic nature of the organization, that the WTO's trade rules were negotiated by member-governments and ratified in members' parliaments. Why, then, should WTO rules be any less democratic than any other decisions of those governments?

It is true that the WTO trade rules were negotiated by member-governments and ratified in members' parliaments, but the interpretations of those rules adopted by the dispute resolution panels and the Appellate Body have not been ratified by those parliaments. While it could be argued that the member-governments knew about the product/process distinction when they agreed, during the Uruguay Round of negotiations, to set up the WTO, the governments had reason to believe that Article XX guaranteed that the agreement into which they were entering would not prevent them from acting in good faith to protect "public morals," "human, animal or plant life or health" or in ways "relating to the conservation of exhaustible natural resources." Subsequently the WTO's Appellate Body interpreted Article XX in a manner that no one could have predicted, virtually emptying it of substantive content. If, in a democracy, a court were to interpret a law in a similar manner, the legislature could revise the law to give effect to its intention. In the case of the WTO, however, since decisions are taken by consensus, it takes only one member-nation in support of the Appellate Body's interpretation of Article XX to block the efforts of other member-nations to change it.

Even if WTO decisions were taken by a majority of the *states* that are members of the WTO, this would still not be a democratic decision-procedure. It would give the democratically elected government of India, representing a billion people, the same number of votes—one—as the democratically elected government of Iceland, representing 275,000. The two may differ in influence in various ways, but there is no formal mechanism for recognizing the difference in population size. In the absence of any means of giving weight to population numbers, the WTO can not be a truly democratic institution.

The Fourth Charge: Taking from the Poor to Give to the Rich

Against the charge that the WTO is a kind of Robin Hood in reverse, President George W. Bush echoed the line taken by most advocates of global free trade when he said in a speech at the World Bank: "Those who protest free trade are no friends of the poor. Those who protest free trade seek to deny them their best hope for escaping poverty."[29] How much truth is there in the claim that free trade, as promoted by the WTO, has helped the world's poorest people?

Although the WTO's critics all agree that the trade body has done more to help huge global corporations than to help the poor, the facts are not easy to sort out, and on some aspects of this question, leading opponents of the WTO do not speak with one voice. Within the covers of a single volume published by the In-

ternational Forum on Globalization, Walden Bello and Vandana
Shiva, based respectively in Thailand and India, say that the rich
nations do not offer a level playing field to the poor nations, and
so free trade does not benefit the South, while Anuradha Mittal,
of the U.S. group Food First, tries to arouse the opposition of
Americans to free trade by showing that free trade between the
United States, Mexico, and Canada has caused hundreds of thousands of U.S. jobs to shift to Mexico and Canada.[30] Since Mexico is a much poorer country than the United States, any transfer
of work from the United States to Mexico can be expected to raise
the income of people who are, on average, much less well off than
those U.S. workers who lose their jobs. Those who favor reducing
poverty globally, rather than only in their own country, should
see this as a good thing.

Another relevant question is whether free trade means cheaper
goods, and whether this is good for the poor. Vandana Shiva, one
of the best-known WTO opponents from one of the less developed countries, writes that the liberalization of trade in India
means that more food is exported, and as a result "food prices
have doubled and the poor have had to cut their consumption in
half." To anyone familiar with poverty in India *before* trade liberalization, it is difficult to believe that India's poor would be able to
survive at all if they had to cut their food consumption in half, so
such claims may well provoke skepticism. That skepticism is not
allayed when one reads, on the very next page, that Indian farmers have lost markets and mills have had to close, because "cheap,
subsidized imports of soybeans are dumped on the Indian market
. . . thus worsening the country's balance of payments situation."[31] If the lowering of trade barriers has meant that soybeans
are now cheaper than they were before, it is strange that this same
lowering of trade barriers should have caused food prices as a
whole to double. Moreover the large quantities of food that Shiva

claims are exported because of trade liberalization should have improved the country's balance of payments. There may be an explanation of such apparently conflicting claims, but if there is, Shiva does not offer it.

In trying to assess the impact of recent trade reforms, it is useful to distinguish two questions:

• Has *inequality* increased during the period of global economic liberalization?
• Have the poor become worse off?

The questions are distinct, because it would be possible for the situation of the poor to improve, in absolute terms—they might eat better, have safer water and greater access to education and health care, and so on—while the situation of the rich improves even more, so that the absolute dollar gap in income and wealth between the rich and the poor is greater than it was when the poor were worse off. (In what follows, unless otherwise specified, I will use "rich" and "poor" to refer to people on high and low incomes, respectively, rather than those with great or small assets. Of course, those with a high income often tend to have a lot of assets, and vice versa. But the correlation is not perfect.) We will also, of course, need to ask whether the changes that can be observed are the result of economic globalization, or merely happen to have coincided with it.

We can begin by describing the present state of poverty in the world. One commonly cited figure, derived from development reports issued by the World Bank and the United Nations, is that of a global population of more than 6 billion, about one-fifth, or 1.2 billion, live on less than $1 per day, and nearly half, or 2.8 billion, live on less than $2 per day. Awful as this sounds, these figures, quoted without further explanation, can be misleading—in the sense of giving the impression that the world's poorest people are not as impoverished as they really are. For we may think to ourselves: the purchasing power of one U.S. dollar in, say, Ethiopia, is vastly greater than the purchasing power of one U.S. dollar in New York. So perhaps these people, though poor, are not as desperately poor as we might imagine? In fact, the figures already take the difference in purchasing power into account. The World Bank's international poverty line—below which these 1.2 billion people fall—is defined as "$1.08 1993 PPP US$" per day, and "PPP" stands for "purchasing power parity." Hence the purchasing power of the daily income of someone right on the World Bank's international poverty line is equivalent to what one could have purchased in the United States in 1993 for $1.08. Granted, there has been some inflation in the United States since 1993, so if we were to express this sum in terms of what can be purchased in the United States in 2000, the figure would rise to $1.28. If we are interested in the actual income of someone living on the poverty line in one of the world's poorest countries—how much their annual earnings would amount to, if they changed them into $US at prevailing exchange rates—we would have to divide this sum by about 4 to take into account the greater purchasing power of $US1 in these countries, as compared with market exchange rates. That yields an actual income of about 32 cents per day. And this figure, remember, is the poverty line itself, in other words, the *upper* bound of a fifth of the world's population. The *average* income of these 1.2 billion people is about 30 percent less, which makes it about 23 cents in U.S. currency at market exchange rates, or the purchasing power equivalent of 92 cents in U.S. currency in the year 2000.[32]

It is not surprising that of these 1.2 billion people, about 826 million lack adequate nutrition, more than 850 million are illiterate, and almost all lack access to even the most basic sanitation. In rich countries, less than one child in a hundred dies before the age of five; in the poorest countries, one in five does. That is 30,000 young children dying every day from preventable causes. Life expectancy in rich nations averages 77, whereas in sub-Saharan Africa it is 48.[33]

This is absolute poverty, which has been described as "a condition of life so characterized by malnutrition, illiteracy, disease, squalid surroundings, high infant mortality and low life expectancy as to be beneath any reasonable definition of human decency."[34] In contrast the average per capita income of the world's wealthiest nations (which contain less than 15 percent of the world's population) is $27,500. This 15 percent of the population divides among itself almost 80 percent of the wealth that the world produces, whereas the assets of the poorest 46 percent of the world's population amount to just 1.25 percent of the world's wealth.[35] The 1999 *Human Development Report* provided an oft-quoted symbol of the far extremities of inequality in the distribution of the world's wealth when it noted that the assets of the world's richest three individuals exceeded the combined Gross National Products of all of the least developed countries, with a population totaling 600 million people.[36]

It is commonly said that inequality between the world's richest and poorest countries has increased during the period in which world trade has increased. Even a 1999 study published by the WTO accepts this view, stating flatly: "It is an empirical fact that the income gap between poor and rich countries has increased in recent decades."[37] According to the widely quoted 1999 *Human Development Report,* in 1820 the fifth of the world's population living in the world's richest countries collectively received three times the combined income of the fifth of the world's population living in the poorest countries. A century later this ratio had increased to 11 to 1. By 1960 it was 30 to 1; by 1990, 60 to 1; and by 1997, 74 to 1.[38] These figures suggest not only an increasing gap between rich nations and poor nations, but an increasing rate of growth in this gap, which grew at an annual rate of 1.66 percent between 1820 and 1960, but between 1990 and 1997 grew at an annual rate of 3 percent.

The 1999 *Human Development Report* figures need to be treated with caution, however, because they are based on comparing incomes at market exchange rates. As we have seen, a given unit of currency may purchase four times as much in a poor country as it could purchase in a rich one, if converted at market exchange rates. When Arne Melchior, Kjetil Telle, and Henrik Wiig, investigating the impact of globalization on inequality for the Norwegian Ministry of Foreign Affairs, adjusted incomes for purchasing power they found that between the 1960s and 1997 there was a continuous decrease in the gap between the average income of the richest nations containing a third of the world's population and the average income of the poorest nations containing a third of the world's population. There was also a small but steady decrease in the gap between the average income of the richest countries containing a fifth of the world's population, and the average income in the poorest countries containing a fifth of the world's population. On the other hand there was an increase in the gap between the average income in the richest countries containing a tenth of the world's population and the poorest countries containing a tenth of the world's population. The reason for the difference between the different sets of comparisons is that in the last three decades the fastest-growing developing countries have not been among the very poorest. Average income in China has grown rapidly and this explains most of the reduction in inequality between the top and bottom thirds. The 2001 *Human Development Report* acknowledged that the Norwegian researchers had got it right, accepting the need to base international comparisons of living standards on purchasing power parity and reporting that on this basis, the ratio of the average income of the richest nations containing a fifth of the world's population to the average income of the poorest nations containing a fifth of the world's population had fallen between 1970 and 1997, from 15 to 1 to 13 to 1, although in the case of the richest 10 percent of nations and the poorest 10 percent of nations, the ratio had grown from 19 to 1 to 27 to 1.[39]

There is, however, a problem even with these figures. As the cumbersome language of the previous paragraph indicates, they compare the average income in rich nations with the average income in poor nations. They are not comparisons of the richest tenth, fifth, or third of the world's population with the poorest tenth, fifth, or third. Obviously, there are some poor people in rich nations, and a few very rich people in poor nations, and when we compare national averages, these intrastate differences could mask the real differences between the world's richest and poorest people. Ideally, we should look at individual household income, rather than national averages. Branko Milanovic, a researcher at the World Bank, has attempted to do this, but the data are much more difficult to obtain. He has compared individual household incomes for two years, 1988 and 1993, and found a sharp increase in inequality between the income of the richest fifth and the poorest fifth of the world's population during these five years.[40] The main reason his results differ from those of Melchior, Telle, and Wiig is that income in urban areas of countries like China and India has risen much faster than income in rural areas. Using national average incomes compresses these urban/rural differences into a single figure. On the other hand, a comparison between just two time-points is not enough to establish a clear trend.

To sum up, although we have quite good data on national per capita average income, that data—on which Melchior, Telle, and Wiig base their study—cannot give us the answer to the right question: Has global income inequality increased? Milanovic, on the other hand, asks the right question, but doesn't have enough data to answer it. As he himself puts it, on the basis of the research he has done so far:

> It is impossible to aver whether inequality is really increasing or whether we see just a temporary spike, or indeed whether the change in the coefficients is statistically significant—bearing in mind numerous and serious data problems.[41]

What really matters? Suppose that the changes Melchior, Telle, and Wiig found hold good for individual incomes, as well as national average incomes. If we are concerned about inequality, should we be pleased to learn that the top and bottom thirds—67 percent of the world's population—have, on average, more equal incomes, if at the same time the top and bottom tenths, amounting to 20 percent of the world's population, have grown even further apart? Different people may have different intuitions about this, but from a broadly utilitarian point of view, these apparently baffling questions do not really raise anything of fundamental importance. Inequality is not significant in itself. It matters because of the impact it has on welfare. We could argue about whether we should be equally concerned with promoting the welfare of all members of society, or whether we should give some kind of priority to promoting the welfare of society's poorest members, but whatever we decide, what matters is people's welfare, and not the size of the gap between rich and poor. Sometimes greater inequality will mean a decrease in overall welfare. There is some evidence that inequality hampers economic growth.[42] Inequality can also undermine the self-esteem of those on the lower levels of society and make them feel worse off than they would be if they were living on the same income in a more egalitarian society.

Sometimes, however, inequality does not matter so greatly. For those who are desperately struggling to get enough to eat and to house and clothe their children, perhaps the need to keep up with one's neighbors is less significant than it is for those who have no difficulty in meeting their basic needs. For people near the bare minimum on which they can survive, a small addition to their income may make a large difference to their welfare, even if their neighbors' incomes grow by much more in dollar terms. So the more important issue about the opening up of world trade may be whether it has made the world's poor worse off than they would otherwise have been, not relative to the rich, but in absolute terms.

Have the poor really have become worse off during the globalization era? On this question the 1997 *Human Development Report* struck a positive note, indicating that poverty has fallen more in the past fifty years than in the previous 500.[43] But the 1999 *Human Development Report* painted a much gloomier picture, showing that on a per capita basis, the Gross Domestic Product of the world's least-developed countries declined by more than 10 percent between 1990 and 1997, from $277 to $245 per annum. Most of these countries are in sub-Saharan Africa, and for that region in general, poverty appears to have increased in recent years, with per capita GDP falling during the same 1990–1997 period from an average per annum of $542 to $518.[44] The 2001 *Human Development Report* combines both the positive and the negative, balancing the 1 percent fall in the already low average incomes in sub-Saharan Africa over the period 1975 to 1999 with the overall rise—almost a doubling—of average incomes in developing countries during the same period. Melchior, Telle, and Wiig paint a similar picture, showing that the average income in the poorest nations containing one-fifth of the world's population more than doubled, when adjusted for purchasing power, between 1965 to 1998, rising from $US551 to $US1137; but in 16 of the world's poorest countries—12 of them in sub-Saharan Africa—average per capita income has fallen. Because of its population size, China's economic improvement plays an important part in the increase in average income in the developing countries.[45]

Income is only one indicator of well-being, and it is helpful to consider others. Life expectancy is obviously an important one. Between 1962 and 1997 average global life expectancy at birth increased from 55 to 66.6 years. Moreover the biggest gain in life expectancy has been in the developing nations, so there has also been a significant decrease in the inequality of life expectancy between nations. In 1960 the average life expectancy for developing countries was only 60 percent of that in the industrial nations. By 1993, it was 82 percent.[46] (But note that, as with income, these figures are national averages, which mask within-country differences that mean greater global differences between individuals.) Life expectancy rose sharply in all regions in the period up to 1987; subsequently it rose much more slowly in Africa, where AIDS has caused life expectancy to fall in some countries, and it has also fallen in Eastern Europe, reflecting the impact of increased poverty following the end of communism.

Food is the most basic need of all, and hence the extent to which people lack it is a crude but useful measure of deprivation. According to the Food and Agriculture Organization, the number of people who are undernourished fell from 960 million in 1969–1971 to 790 million in 1995–1997. This decrease may seem like very modest progress over a quarter of a century, but taking into account the growth in world population during this period, it means that the proportion of people who are undernourished has fallen from 37 percent to 18 percent.[47]

Each year the United Nations Development Program reports

on each country's progress in terms of a composite measure called the Human Development Index, based on a combination of indicators for income, life expectancy, and education. The Human Development Index scores for the developing countries, and also for the least developed countries, considered separately, have risen consistently between 1960 and 1993, suggesting that the world's poorer people have become better off overall in terms of income, life expectancy, and the amount of education they receive.[48]

Globally, the World Bank estimates that the number of people living below the international poverty line has risen slightly since 1987.[49] But should the increase in absolute numbers be taken as a sign that poverty is getting worse, or the decrease in the proportion of the population who are poor as a sign that things are improving? One could argue either way. Life below the poverty line is so lacking in the basic necessities for a decent life that it is a bad thing that anyone has to subsist in these conditions. Yet if human life, when some minimum requirements are satisfied, is a good thing—and it takes a serious pessimist to deny that—then we should be pleased that there are more human beings living above the poverty line, and the diminishing fraction of the total population forced to live below that line can be seen as a good thing. To go further into the choice between these differing value judgments would lead us into deep philosophical issues and take us far from the themes of this book, so here it will be enough merely to note that both views have something to be said for them. We can then move on to our final question: Is there a causal link between poverty and economic globalization?[50]

On theoretical grounds, as we have seen, there is some reason to believe that open markets and free trade should increase economic welfare as a whole. The theory finds some support in an Organization for Economic Cooperation and Development (OECD) study showing that when corporations go into foreign countries, they generally pay more than the national average wage.[51] But information about average wages does not alleviate concerns about poverty, as long as inequality is increasing. We have seen that whether global inequality has increased during the era of expanding world trade is still highly contentious. We don't have the household income data we would need to get a well-grounded answer. Since a correlation does not show a causal connection, even if we had all the data we needed on trends in global income distribution, and even if these data showed rising inequality and poverty, it would still be difficult to judge whether economic globalization has contributed to any increase that might have occurred in economic inequality and in the number of people living in poverty. Consider, as illustrating the difficulty of the problem, the following three expert opinions.

Peter Lindert and Jeffrey Williamson have studied the connection between inequality and globalization for the National Bureau of Economic Research, in Cambridge, Massachusetts. They are among those who accept that as the global economy has become more integrated over the past two centuries, so too economic inequality between nations has increased. In their view, however, globalization has not brought about this widening income gap. On the contrary, without globalization the rise in inequality would have been greater still. Their figures indicate that in Third World countries between 1973 and 1992, per capita Gross Domestic Product rose fastest in those countries strongly open to trade, rose more slowly in countries moderately open to trade, and actually fell in countries that were hostile to trade. They summarize their conclusion by saying that "world incomes would still be unequal under complete global integration, as they are in any large integrated national economy. But they would be less unequal in a fully integrated world economy than in one fully segmented."[52]

World Bank researchers Mattias Lundberg and Lyn Squire used a sample of 38 countries to assess the impact of openness to global trade on economic gains for different sections of the population. They found that globalization benefits the majority, but its burden falls on poorest 40 percent, for whom openness leads to a fall in economic growth. They conclude: "At least in the short run, globalization appears to increase poverty and inequality."[53]

The Norwegian team of Melchior, Telle, and Wiig hold, as we have seen, that when measured in particular ways, income inequality has decreased during the era of more open world trade. But they do not think that the data permit one to conclude that globalization reduces inequality. It is difficult to disentangle the impact of technological change from the impact of globalization, as the two have occurred in tandem—and are indeed interrelated. There is some evidence that technological change increases inequality between highly skilled workers, who can make use of new technologies, and unskilled workers, whose labor the new technologies may make redundant. Political changes are also important. There is a clear connection between the collapse of communism and the decline in average income and even in life expectancy in much of Eastern Europe during the 1990s, and in some countries in sub-Saharan Africa the lack of a stable and effective government can make progress impossible.[54] (The disastrous situation of the Congo, which by 2001 was probably the world's poorest nation, is in large part the outcome of prolonged conflict there.[55])

With so many different ways of assessing inequality, and so many different findings, what is the ordinary citizen to think? No evidence that I have found enables me to form a clear view about the overall impact of economic globalization on the poor. Most likely, it has helped some to escape poverty and thrown others deeper into it; but whether it has helped more people than it has harmed and whether it has caused more good to those it has helped than it has brought misery to those it has harmed is something that, without better data, we just cannot know.

Judgment

We have now considered the four charges commonly made against the WTO. We found that, first, the WTO does, through its use of the product/process rule and its very narrow interpretation of Article XX, place economic considerations ahead of concerns for other issues, such as environmental protection and animal welfare, that arise from how the product is made. If the human rights of the workers were violated in the process of making the product, this would presumably be treated in a similar manner, if a complaint were made. Second, while the WTO does not violate national sovereignty in any formal sense, the operations of the WTO do in practice reduce the scope of national sovereignty. The WTO's defense to this charge, that the governments of member-nations have voluntarily opted for this curtailment, is weakened by the surprising interpretation its Appellate Body has given to Article XX; but even if this were not the case, and the member-nations had fully understood how the treaty they were signing would operate, it would still be the case that WTO membership curtails national sovereignty in the sense that, in the real world, it is often hard to leave the WTO and as long as it remains a member, a country's power to make some important decisions is eroded. Third, the WTO is undemocratic both in theory and practice, firstly because a procedure requiring unanimous consent to any change is not a form of democracy, secondly because the dispute panels and the Appellate Body are not responsible to either the majority of members or the majority of the planet's adult population, and thirdly because the organization is disproportionately influenced by the major trading powers. On the fourth, and arguably most important charge against the WTO, however, that it makes the rich richer and the poor poorer, the verdict has to be: not proven. The available evidence is insufficient to convict either globalization or the WTO of that charge.

This assessment of the charges against the WTO is based on the organization's actions up to the time of the 2001 ministerial meeting at Doha, the first WTO ministerial meeting since the protests in Seattle. The declarations agreed to at that meeting display a new concern for the interests of developing countries, including the world's poorest countries, and a willingness to consider other values as a constraint on what had hitherto been the overriding value of free trade. It will be several years before we know whether these declarations were merely good public relations or a sign of a substantial change in the thinking of the WTO that will make a real difference.

Can Do Better?

In the *Communist Manifesto,* Karl Marx described the impact of the capitalist class in terms that might today be applied to the WTO:

It has resolved personal worth into exchange value, and in place of the numberless indefeasible chartered freedoms, has set up that single, unconscionable freedom—Free Trade. . . . All fixed, fast-frozen relations, with their train of ancient and venerable prejudices and opinions are swept away, all new-formed ones become antiquated before they can ossify. All that is solid melts into air, all that is holy is profaned.[56]

Defenders of the WTO would reject loaded words like "unconscionable" but might otherwise accept this account of what they are seeking to achieve. That free trade is a goal of overriding importance is implicit in the decisions of the WTO dispute panels. They would also agree that a global free market will sweep away "ancient and venerable prejudices" and they would see this as a good thing, because such prejudices restrict the use of individual creativity that brings benefits both to the innovative producer and to the consumers who can choose to take advantage of it.

Whether we accept or reject the claim that economic globalization is a good thing, we can still ask if there are ways of making it work better, or at least less badly. Even those who accept the general argument for the economic benefits of a global free market should ask themselves how well a global free market can work in the absence of any global authority to set minimum standards on issues like child labor, worker safety, the right to form a union, and environmental and animal welfare protection.

According to standard economic models, if various assumptions hold—including the assumptions that people always act fully rationally and on the basis of perfect information—free trade within a single, well-governed nation can be expected to create a state of affairs that is "Pareto efficient"—in other words, a state of affairs where no one's welfare can be improved without reducing the welfare of at least one other person. This is because the government will have legislated so that the private costs of production are brought into line with their costs to society overall. A corporation that pollutes a river into which it discharges wastes will be made to clean it up and to compensate those who have been harmed. Thus the costs of keeping the environment clean become part of the costs of production—in economic jargon, they are "internalized"—and producers who try to save money by not cleaning up their wastes gain no economic advantages over their competitors. But when we consider global free trade in the absence of any global authority to regulate pollution, or any civil law that provides remedies to the victims of pollution, the situation is different. A national government may have little interest in forcing a producer to internalize damage done to the global environment, for example to the oceans or the atmosphere or to stocks of cetaceans, fish, or migrating birds. Even though all nations share the global environment, the "tragedy of the commons" rules here, and a nation may benefit more by allowing its fishing fleet to catch as much as it can than by restraining the fleet so that the fleets of other nations can catch more. Thus, judged strictly in economic terms, without global environmental protection there is no reason to expect free trade to be Pareto efficient, let alone to maximize overall welfare.

Even if we ignore goods that belong to no nation, and focus on the quality of life in each nation, since governments are imperfect, unconstrained globalization is likely to lead to economic inefficiencies. If a ruling elite does not care about the working classes, or about the people of a particular region of its territory, it may not take into account the cost to them of air or water pollution, or for that matter of being forced to work long hours for little pay. Countries governed by such elites can then out-compete countries that provide some minimal conditions for their workers and, as Herman Daly puts it, "more of world production shifts to countries that do the poorest job of counting costs—a sure recipe for reducing the efficiency of global production."[57] The result is that the nexus between human welfare and the growth of the global economy, incomplete at the best of times, will be further eroded.

Significantly, the desirability of uniform global environmental and labor standards is a point on which critics of the WTO from the poorer countries often differ with labor and environmental activists from the rich countries. The fear is that the rich countries will use high standards to keep out goods from the poor countries. Vandana Shiva claims "social clauses make bed-fellows of Northern trade unions and their corporations to jointly police and undermine social movements in the South."[58] There is no doubt that this could happen, but what is the alternative? Various measures could be taken to give developing countries more time to adjust, but in the end, just as national laws and regulations were eventually seen as essential to prevent the inhuman harshness of nineteenth century laissez-faire capitalism in the industrialized nations, so instituting global standards is the only way to prevent an equally inhuman form of uncontrolled global capitalism. The WTO accepts this idea, at least in theory. At its 1996 Ministerial meeting in Singapore, the WTO ministers renewed an earlier commitment "to the observance of internationally recognized core labor standards" and affirmed its support for the International Labor Organization as the body to set these standards. In Doha in 2001 the ministers reaffirmed that declaration and noted the "work under way in the International Labor Organization (ILO) on the social dimension of globalization."[59] Unfortunately nothing concrete had happened in the five years between those statements.

The WTO has up to now been dominated by neoliberal economic thinking. With some signs that the WTO is willing to rethink this approach, it is possible to imagine a reformed WTO in which the overwhelming commitment to free trade is replaced by a commitment to more fundamental goals. The WTO could then become a tool for pursuing these objectives. There are even clauses in the GATT agreement that could become the basis for affirmative action in trade, designed to help the least developed nations. In article XXXVI (3) the contracting parties agree that there is a "need for positive efforts designed to ensure that less-developed contracting parties secure a share in the growth in international trade commensurate with the needs of their economic development."[60] Under the present WTO regime, such clauses have been nice-sounding words with no practical impact. Far from making positive efforts to help the less-developed nations, the rich nations, especially the United States and the European Union, have failed to do even their fair share of reducing their own trade barriers in those areas that would do most good for the less developed nations. As *The Economist*—usually an avid supporter of the WTO—has reported, "Rich countries cut their tariffs by less in the Uruguay Round than poor ones did. Since then they have found new ways to close their markets."[61] The *New York Times* has said that several protectionist measures in the richest countries "mock those countries' rhetorical support for free trade."[62] Rich countries impose tariffs on manufactured goods from poor countries that are, according to one study, four times as high as those they impose on imports from other rich countries.[63] The WTO itself has pointed out that the rich nations subsidize their agricultural producers at a rate of $1 billion a day, or more than six times the level of development aid they give to poor nations.[64]

As we have already noted, there were signs at the November 2001 WTO meeting that the criticisms of the WTO are having some effect. If the WTO begins to take seriously GATT articles like XXXVI (3), we could in time come to see the WTO as a platform from which a policy of laissez-faire in global trade could be replaced by a more democratically controlled system of regulation that promotes minimum standards for environmental protection, worker safety, union rights, and animal welfare. But if the WTO cannot respond to these influences, it would be best for its scope to be curtailed by a body willing to take on the challenges of setting global environmental and social standards and finding ways of making them stick.

Trade, Legitimacy, and Democracy

We tend to think of trade as something politically neutral. In trading with a country, governments do not think that they are taking an ethical stand. They often trade with countries while disapproving of their regimes. In extreme cases, this neutrality breaks down. Many corporations and some governments recognized that doing business with South Africa under apartheid raised serious moral questions. Normally, however, governments keep the question of whether they should trade with a country separate from the question of whether they approve of its government. The United States has attacked China for its human rights record while at the same time expanding its trade with China. But sometimes trading with a country implies an ethical judgment. Many trade deals are done with governments. This is especially likely to be the case when transnational corporations make arrangements with the governments of developing countries to explore for oil and minerals, to cut timber, to fish, or to build big hotels and develop tourist complexes. Nigeria, for example, gets more than $6 billion a year, or about a quarter of its Gross Domestic Product, from selling oil. When multinational corporations like Shell trade with governments like those that Nigeria has had for most of the past thirty years—that is, military dictatorships—they are implicitly accepting the government's right to sell the resources that lie within its borders. What gives a government the moral right to sell the resources of the country over which it rules? [65]

The same question can be asked about international borrowing privileges. Corrupt dictators are allowed to borrow money from foreign countries or international lending bodies, and if they should happen to be overthrown, then the next government is seen as obliged by the signature of its predecessor to repay the loan. Should it refuse to do so, it will be excluded from international financial institutions and suffer adverse consequences. No questions are asked by the lenders about whether this or that dictator is entitled to borrow in the name of his or her country. Effective control of a territory is seen as being enough to obviate any inquiry into how that person came by that degree of control.

Both the conventional moral view, and the view taken in international law, is that once a government is recognized as legitimate, that legitimacy automatically confers the right to trade in the country's resources. The plausibility of this answer rests in the assertion that the government that is doing the trading is "legitimate." That sounds like a term that expresses an ethical judgment about the right of the government to hold power. If this were so, then the answer to the challenge to the government's right to trade in the country's resources would be: a government that satisfies certain ethical standards regarding its claim to rule has the right to trade in the resources of the country over which it rules. But in fact that is not what is usually meant by calling a government "legitimate." The standard view has long been that the recognition of a government as legitimate has nothing to do with how that government came to power, or for that matter with how it governs. "The Law of Nations prescribes no rules as regards the kind of head a State may have," wrote Lassa Oppenheim in his influential 1905 text on international law, and he added that every state is "naturally" free to adopt any constitution "according to its discretion."[66] The sole test is whether it is in effective control of the territory. More recently Roth has put it this way:

> In such a conception, the international system regards
> ruling apparatuses as self-sufficient sources of authority—

or rather deems their authority to derive from their
characteristic ability to secure the acquiescence of their
populaces, by whatever means . . . a government is
recognized simply because its existence is a fact of life.[67]

International bodies, including the United Nations and the
World Trade Organization, use this concept of legitimacy when
they accept governments as the representatives of member nations.

The dominance of this conception makes alternatives seem
unrealistic. There is, however, an alternative view with strong
ethical credentials. In November 1792, in the wake of the French
National Convention's declaration of a republic, Thomas Jefferson, then U.S. Secretary of State, wrote to the representative of
the United States in France: "It accords with our principles to ac-
knowledge any government to be rightful which is formed by the
will of the people, substantially declared."[68] Now it is true that
we cannot assume, from this statement, that Jefferson also intended the converse: that a government that cannot show that it
has been formed by the declared will of the people is not right-
fully the government of the nation. There may well be other
grounds on which a government could be considered legitimate,
perhaps by ruling unopposed for a long period without employing repressive measures to stifle dissent. The Jeffersonian principle does seem to imply, however, that some governments would
not be regarded as legitimate—for example, one that had seized
power by force of arms, dismissed democratically elected rulers,
and killed those who spoke out against this way of doing things.

The claim that there is a fundamental human right to take part
in deciding who governs us provides one reason for denying the
legitimacy of a government that cannot show that it represents
the will of the people. We could reach the same conclusion by ar-

guing, on consequentialist grounds, that democratic governments can be expected to have more concern for the people over
whom they rule than governments that do not answer, at regular
intervals, to an electorate. In international law, this view of legitimacy has been gathering support in recent years, although it
could not yet be said to be the majority view. In support of it, its
defenders can point to many international documents, beginning with the opening words of the United Nations Charter, "We
the peoples." The signatories of the Charter apparently regarded
themselves as representatives of, and deriving their authority
from, the peoples they governed. Next comes the Universal Declaration of Human Rights, which in Article 21 (3) states:

> The will of the people shall be the basis of the authority of
> government; this will shall be expressed in periodic and
> genuine elections which shall be by universal and equal
> suffrage and shall be held by secret vote or by equivalent
> free voting procedures.

The Universal Declaration of Human Rights is not a treaty
with explicit legal force, but the International Covenant on Civil
and Political Rights is. Its first article states:

> All peoples have the right of self-determination. By virtue
> of that right they freely determine their political status and
> freely pursue their economic, social and cultural
> development.

In the second article, the parties to the Covenant undertake to
ensure that each individual in its territory has the rights it con-
tains "without distinction of any kind, such as race, color, sex,
language, religion, political or other opinion, national or social
origin, property, birth or other status." The inclusion of "political
or other opinion" is important here, since Article 25 reads:

Every citizen shall have the right and the opportunity, without any of the distinctions mentioned in article 2 and without unreasonable restrictions:
(a) To take part in the conduct of public affairs, directly or through freely chosen representatives;
(b) To vote and to be elected at genuine periodic elections which shall be by universal and equal suffrage and shall be held by secret ballot, guaranteeing the free expression of the will of the electors.

If we were to take these statements seriously, we would have to develop an entirely new concept of legitimate government, with far-reaching implications not only for trade but also for issues like the use of military intervention for humanitarian purposes, a topic to which I shall turn in the next chapter. But how would we decide when a government is sufficiently democratic to be recognized as legitimate? During the counting and recounting of votes in the United States presidential election in November 2000, jokes circulated to the effect that the United Nations was about to send in a team of observers to ensure that the elections were fair and democratic. The jokes had a serious point to make. Put aside the many allegations of irregularities in voting and counting and the refusal of the United States Supreme Court to allow a proper count of all votes. Forget about the fact that candidates must raise hundreds of millions of dollars to have any chance of success, thus ensuring that the rich have far more influence on the political process than the poor. Even without any of those blemishes, the use of the electoral college, rather than the popular vote, to elect the president of the United States gives greater value to the votes of people living in states with small populations than to those living in states with large populations, and hence fails the basic "one vote, one value" requirement of democracy, and the

"equal suffrage" stipulation of Article 25 (b) of the Universal Declaration of Human Rights. Nevertheless, the evident imperfec-
tions of democracy in the United States are not of the kind that
should lead us to withdraw recognition of the legitimacy of the
U.S. government. A minimalist concept of democracy is needed,
for otherwise there will be few legitimate governments left. It
may be useful to distinguish between governments that, although
not democratic, can claim a traditional, long-standing authority
that enables them to rule with the apparent acquiescence of the
population, and without severe restrictions on basic civil liber-
ties, and other regimes that, having seized power by force, use repressive measures to maintain themselves in power. A traditional
absolute monarchy might be an example of the first form of government; a military regime that has come to power through a successful coup, does not hold free elections, and kills or jails its opponents is an example of the second.

Even if we focus only on those governments that gain power by
force and hold it through repression of opposition, accepting the
democratic concept of sovereignty would make a huge difference
to the way we conduct world affairs. With regard to trade issues,
we can imagine that an internationally respected body would ap-
point a tribunal consisting of judges and experts to scrutinize the
credentials of each government on a regular basis. If a government could not, over time, satisfy the tribunal that its legitimacy
stemmed from the support of its people, it would not be accepted
as having the right to sell its country's resources, any more than
a robber who overpowers you and takes your watch would be
recognized as entitled to sell it. For a private citizen to buy that
watch, knowing or reasonably suspecting it to be stolen, is to
commit the crime of receiving stolen goods. Under a minimalist
democratic concept of sovereignty, it would similarly be a crime
under international law for anyone to receive goods stolen from a

nation by those who have no claim to sovereignty other than the fact that they exercise superior force.

Far-reaching as they are, such suggestions are gaining increasing recognition. At the Summit of the Americas meeting held in Quebec City in April 2001, the leaders of 34 American nations agreed that "any unconstitutional alteration or interruption of the democratic order in a state of the hemisphere constitutes an insurmountable obstacle to the participation of that state's government in the Summit of the Americas process." This means that a country that ceases to be a democracy cannot take part in the continuing talks on the free trade pact that the Summit planned, nor receive support from major international institutions like the Inter-American Development Bank.[69] In other words, democracy takes precedence over free trade, and the perceived benefits of participation in the proposed free trade agreement provide an incentive for all the nations of the Americas to maintain democratic institutions.

Though most leaders present at the Summit of the Americas, including President George W. Bush, are strong defenders of free trade and of the WTO, there is a potential conflict between the vision implicit in their Quebec City agreement and that of the WTO. The leaders of the nations of the Americas envision a kind of club of democratic nations, who trade with each other, assist each other in various ways, and deny these benefits to undemocratic outsiders or to any democracies that fall into the hands of dictators. In contrast the rules of the WTO do not allow its member nations to refuse to trade with other members because they are not democratic. If the WTO should realize its vision of a global free trade zone, regional free trade agreements would become irrelevant, and there would be no way in which trade sanctions could encourage democracy.

In Europe the lure of entry into the European Union is already encouraging democracy and support for basic human rights. For the former communist nations of Central and Eastern Europe, membership in the European Union is an extremely desirable goal, one that is likely to bring with it stability and prosperity. The European Union is a free trade zone, but it is much more than that. It has criteria for admission that include a democratic form of government and basic human rights guarantees.[70] Implicitly, by refusing to accept nations that fail to meet these standards, the European Union puts democracy and human rights ahead of free trade. As a result, those Central and Eastern European nations that are plausible candidates for membership are gradually bringing their laws in line with the minimum standards required by the European Union.

It is not only in Europe and the Americas that there are moves to strengthen and encourage democracy. In Africa, there has been increasing acceptance of the monitoring of elections by international observers, and the Organization of African Unity has now monitored elections in 39 countries.[71] At the inaugural meeting of the Community of Democracies in Warsaw in June 2000, representatives of the governments of 106 countries signed the *Warsaw Declaration,* recognizing "the universality of democratic values," and agreeing to "collaborate on democracy-related issues in existing international and regional institutions, forming coalitions and caucuses to support resolutions and other international activities aimed at the promotion of democratic governance" in order to "create an external environment conducive to democratic development."[72] Here too democracy is seen as a great value, to be promoted through international collaboration. A trade pact between democracies, like that proposed for the Americas, would be a powerful means of promoting the value of democracy. So too would be a blacklist of illegitimate governments with no color of entitlement to rule, and with whom there is therefore no ethical basis for doing business. Corporations that wished to be perceived, not as the receivers of stolen goods, but as respectable global citizens and as supporters of democracy, might then be deterred from entering into agreements with these governments. This result would deny dictators the resources they need for buying weapons, paying their supporters, and boosting their bank balances in Switzerland. Obtaining power by ways that do not confer legitimacy would become just a little less attractive, and the prospects of an illegitimate government staying in power would be slightly reduced. Though the reduced prospects of development might be seen as a cost incurred not only by the illegitimate government but also by the people of the country, such development is, at best, a mixed blessing, and is often very damaging to the local people. For example, Shell's use of oil rights under the regime of the former Nigerian dictator General Sani Abacha was highly detrimental to the Ogoni people who lived above the oil fields. It can also be argued that it was, on balance, bad for Nigeria as a whole. In a study of the impact of extractive industries on the poor, Michael Ross, a political scientist at the University of California, Los Angeles, found that the living standards and quality of life experienced by the general population in countries dependent on selling minerals and oil are much lower than one would expect them to be, given the countries' per capita income. Mineral dependence correlated strongly with high levels of poverty and with unusually high levels of corruption, authoritarian government, military spending, and civil war. Ross's findings are in accord with those of an earlier influential study of natural resources and economic growth by Jeffrey Sachs and Andrew Warner.[73]

Consistently with such studies, we may think it is no coincidence that Nigeria has over the last 30 years had a preponderance of military governments, one of the world's highest levels of corruption, and enormous revenue from the sale of oil. Control of such vast wealth is a constant temptation for generals and others who have the means to overthrow civilian governments and then divert some of the wealth into their own pockets. If overthrowing the government did not bring with it control of the oil revenues, the temptation to do so would be that much less.[74]

A refusal to accept a dictatorial government as entitled to sell off the resources of the country over which it rules is not the same as the imposition of a total trade boycott on that country. Such boycotts can be very harmful to individual citizens in the country boycotted. Renewable resources, like agricultural produce and manufactured goods, might still be traded under private agreements. But when a corporation or a nation accepts the right of dictators to sell their country's non-renewable natural resources, it is accepting the dictators' claims to legitimate authority over those resources. This is not a neutral act, but one that requires ethical justification. In the rare case in which the dictatorship's record indicates that the money will be used to benefit the entire nation, that justification may be available, despite the absence of democracy. When, however, corporations can see that the money they are paying for a country's natural resources will be used primarily to enrich its dictator and enable him or her to buy more arms to consolidate his or her rule, there is no ethical justification for dealing with the dictator. The old-growth forests, oil, and minerals should be left alone, awaiting a government that has legitimate authority to sell them.

4 one law

The Need for Intervention

We have seen how increased awareness of our dependence on the shared and vulnerable atmosphere of our planet and the movement toward a more integrated world economy have both put pressure on traditional ideas of state sovereignty. There is another area in which the traditional idea of state sovereignty has been more directly confronted—and overridden. Support for an effective universal prohibition on genocide and crimes against humanity shows more clearly than any other issue how our conception of the sovereign rights of states has changed over the past 50 years. This chapter examines why that has happened, how it has been defended, and why it is justified.

Genocide is not a new phenomenon. Anyone who has read the Bible knows that. The *Book of Numbers* tells of a time when Israelite men were succumbing to the charms of the women of a neighboring tribe, the Midianites. Worse still, it seems that these

women succeeded in persuading their Israelite lovers to follow
the Midianite religion:

> And the LORD spake unto Moses, saying, Avenge the
> children of Israel of the Midianites. And Moses spake unto
> the people, saying, Arm some of yourselves unto the war,
> and let them go against the Midianites, and avenge the
> LORD of Midian. Of every tribe a thousand, throughout
> all the tribes of Israel, shall ye send to the war. So there
> were delivered out of the thousands of Israel, a thousand of
> every tribe, twelve thousand armed for war. . . . And they
> warred against the Midianites, as the LORD commanded
> Moses; and they slew all the males. . . . And the children of
> Israel took all the women of Midian captives, and their
> little ones, and took the spoil of all their cattle, and all their
> flocks, and all their goods. And they burnt all their cities
> wherein they dwelt, and all their goodly castles, with fire.
> And they took all the spoil, and all the prey, both of men
> and of beasts. And they brought the captives, and the prey,
> and the spoil, unto Moses, and Eleazar the priest, and unto
> the congregation of the children of Israel, unto the camp at
> the plains of Moab, which are by Jordan near Jericho. And
> Moses, and Eleazar the priest, and all the princes of the
> congregation, went forth to meet them without the camp.
> And Moses was wroth with the officers of the host, with
> the captains over thousands, and captains over hundreds,
> which came from the battle. And Moses said unto them,
> Have ye saved all the women alive? Behold, these caused
> the children of Israel . . . to commit trespass against the
> LORD . . . and there was a plague among the congregation
> of the LORD. Now therefore kill every male among the
> little ones, and kill every woman that hath known man by

lying with him. But all the women children, that have not known a man by lying with him, keep alive for yourselves.[1]

For much of the past century it has been widely believed that people commit crimes of violence because they are poor, ignorant, oppressed, abused, or exploited; or if none of these adjectives apply to them at the time they commit these crimes, then one or more of them must have applied to them at a formative period of their individual psyche, such as their childhood. This was supposed to be true not only of people who commit individual crimes but also of those who take part in crimes on a larger scale. It follows from this view that trying to prevent crimes by more effective policing is treating the symptoms and not the causes. To get at the roots of the problem we must end injustice and exploitation, improve and reform education so that it teaches the importance of respecting our fellow human beings, irrespective of race, religion, or politics, prevent the corruption of the democratic process by the arms manufacturers and others who profit from war or genocide, and ensure that no child is brought up in poverty or by abusive parents.

We would, I hope, all like to end injustice and exploitation, and see that no child lives in poverty or is abused. Nor would I disagree with those who would like to see our schools do whatever they can to encourage an attitude of respect for others. Perhaps doing these things would reduce violence, but we ought to do them even if it does nothing to reduce violence. But would doing them be enough to put an end to violence, and make other measures unnecessary? I do not think so, and the passage from the *Book of Numbers* that I have quoted suggests three reasons why it will not.

First, that text—especially if read alongside other biblical passages describing other slaughters, no less ruthless[2]—shows that the horrific mass killings of the twentieth century were not a new phenomenon, except insofar as modern technology and communications enabled the killers to murder far more people in a relatively brief period of time than had ever happened before. As Lawrence Keeley has shown in *War Before Civilization,* war has been a regular part of the existence of the overwhelming majority of human cultures, and male prisoners were usually not taken, although women and children sometimes were. Massacres of entire groups seem not to have been unusual. The mass graves of Europe—burial pits containing people of all ages who have met violent deaths—go back at least 7,000 years, to the Neolithic grave at Talheim, in Germany. At Crow Creek, in South Dakota, more than a century before Columbus sailed for America, 500 men, women, and children were scalped and mutilated before being thrown into a ditch. It is a sobering thought that in many tribal societies, despite the absence of machine guns and high explosives, the percentage of the population killed annually in warfare far exceeds that of any modern society, including Germany and Russia in the twentieth century.[3]

Second, the text clearly suggests that the Israelite motivation for wiping out the Midianites had nothing to do with their own poverty, nor with any injustice they had suffered at the hands of the people they attacked. In fact the Midianites appear to have committed no crime at all except consenting to sexual relations —to which, presumably, the Israelite men also consented—and having a religion that was, at least to some Israelites, more attractive than that followed by Moses.

Third, if the Lord had not spoken of vengeance, but had given Moses a modern genetics textbook and commanded him to do whatever would maximize the number of Israelite descendants, then Moses might have acted exactly as he is portrayed as doing in *Numbers.* Since women can have only a limited number of chil-

dren, and the Israelite men were capable of providing them with
all the sperm they need for that purpose, Midianite males were
potential competitors and of no genetic use to the Israelites. So
Moses ruthlessly eliminated them, men and boys alike. Killing all
the Midianite women who are not virgins ensured that there were
no pregnant women who might carry male Midianite children,
and it was an effective way of ensuring that there would be no one
of full Midianite descent in the next generation. Allowing the
captains to keep the young Midianite females for themselves increased the number of their own descendants.

Here we have an example of genocide in which the genetic advantage to the perpetrators is as clear as anything can be. What
does this mean for us? We are all the descendants of men who succeeded in leaving their genes in subsequent generations, while
many other men did not. Killing rival males with whom one does
not share any genes and mating with their wives or daughters is
one way in which men can, when the circumstances allow, en-
hance their prospects of leaving their genes in subsequent generations. Don't be misled by the thought that the killing of some
humans by others cannot be good for the species. Species come in
and out of existence too slowly to be the dominant unit of evolution. It is better to think of evolution as a competition between
genes, individuals, and perhaps small, genetically related groups,
than between species. That, presumably, has something to do
with the central part that war and massacre have played in human
history and pre-history. Indeed, the capacity to commit massacres probably goes back even further than our distinct identity
as human beings. Chimpanzees, who together with bonobos are
our closest non-human relatives, go on raiding parties across the
borders of their territory in which they deliberately—if you
doubt that word, read a description of how they go about it—
seek out and kill vulnerable chimpanzees, usually males, from an-

other group. In one instance the chimpanzees that Jane Goodall was observing at Gombe completely wiped out a neighboring group over a three-year period, killing at least four adult and adolescent males and one adult female, driving away all the other adults, and "keeping alive for themselves," if I may here use the biblical expression, the two young daughters of the adult female they had killed. Similar behavior has been observed in other chimpanzee groups widely dispersed across Africa.[4]

Are we, then, all potential perpetrators of genocide? That goes too far. There are many ways in which one can do better than others in leaving one's genes in later generations. One of them is being particularly good at forming mutually beneficial cooperative relationships.[5] Amazingly, humans can do this even when they are divided into warring nations, marched into trenches facing each other, given a rifle, and told to kill the enemy in the other trenches.[6] The circumstances in which this is likely to be advantageous are more common than the circumstances in which genocide is likely to be advantageous. Thus we could say that we are all potential cooperators. But that a significant number of human males have the potential to be perpetrators of genocide is, in view of the evidence from ethology, anthropology, and history, highly plausible. It is also plausible to believe that although this potential may be more likely to be acted upon in the presence of poverty, injustice, exploitation, or a lack of education, it may also be acted upon without these factors.

If we bring our gaze forward from biblical times to the century that has just ended, we find terrible confirmation of that bleak statement. In 1915 to 1917 Turks massacred perhaps 1.5 million Armenians. In the 1930s Stalin ordered the deaths of somewhere between 7 and 10 million people. The figure of 6 million is usually assigned to the Nazi genocide against Jews. Then came the killings in Cambodia, in Rwanda, and as the century neared its end, in Bosnia, Kosovo, and East Timor. Some of these killings were perpetrated by people who were poor and uneducated, but others were not. Germany in the 1920s was among the most highly educated nations in the world. Yugoslavia had, since 1918, been striving to educate its citizens to think of themselves as Yugoslavs, not as Croats, Serbs, or members of other nationalities or ethnic groups. Timothy Garton Ash asks, in his *History of the Present,* What have we learned from the events in that region during the last decade of the twentieth century? He answers: "We have learned that human nature has not changed. That Europe at the end of the twentieth century is quite as capable of barbarism as it was in the Holocaust of mid-century."[7] He might have also said: and for millennia before that, and not only in Europe.

So although overcoming poverty, eliminating injustice, and improving education may make genocide less likely, we cannot rely on these policies alone to prevent it. What else can be done? Developing mechanisms to promote peace and reduce the risk of war between nations is important, for the mentality of war breaks down inhibitions and makes men more prone to kill noncombatants as well as the enemy's armed forces. But in the end, we need to be able to do something that will make potential perpetrators of genocide fear the consequences of their actions. Just as, at the domestic level, the last line of defense against individual crimes of murder, rape, and assault is law enforcement, so too the last line of defense against genocide and similar crimes must be law enforcement, at a global level, and where other methods of achieving that fail, the method of last resort will be military intervention.

The Development of International Criminal Law

The charter of the International Military Tribunal set up by the Allies to try the leading Nazi war criminals at Nuremberg gave it jurisdiction over three kinds of crimes: crimes against peace, war crimes, and crimes against humanity. In promulgating this charter, the Allies declared it a "crime against peace" to initiate a war of aggression; a "war crime" to murder, ill-treat, or deport either civilians or prisoners of war; and a "crime against humanity" to murder, exterminate, enslave, or deport any civilian population, or to persecute them on political, racial, or religious grounds. These acts, the charter of the tribunal stated, are crimes "whether or not in violation of the domestic law of the country where perpetrated."[8]

Though the Allies were able to draw on earlier precedents and conventions to justify their claim that crimes against humanity were already recognized in international law, the Nuremberg Tribunal gave new impetus to the idea that certain acts are so horrendous that they are crimes, no matter what the prevailing law at the time in the country in which they are perpetrated. Subsequently the United Nations General Assembly asked the International Law Commission to formulate principles of international law relating to crimes such as those dealt with by the Nuremberg Tribunal and the Commission recommended that there should be international criminal responsibility for crimes against humanity committed at the instigation or with the toleration of state authorities. The 1984 Convention against Torture, signed by 110 states, accepted this principle. That Convention was central to the House of Lords decision on whether the United Kingdom government could extradite Senator Auguste Pinochet to Spain, to be tried there for crimes he was alleged to have committed in Chile. Chile had ratified the Convention against Torture, and this was sufficient for the law lords to find that Pinochet could be extradited to Spain.[9] But that case also raised the question of what is called "universal jurisdiction," that is, the right of any country to try a person who has committed crimes against hu-

manity, irrespective of whether the country in which the crime
was committed is a signatory to a convention that provides for international criminal responsibility in respect of that crime.

At the time of the Pinochet hearing, Amnesty International
made a strong case that international law recognizes universal jurisdiction for crimes of humanity.[10] The prosecution of Adolf
Eichmann in Israel is often cited as a precedent for this view.[11]
Eichmann was, under Himmler and Heydrich, in charge of the
implementation of the murder of European Jews under Nazi
rule. He was kidnapped in Argentina and flown to Israel, where
he was tried and subsequently executed. Though the method by
which he was brought to Israel was of doubtful legality, there has
been general acceptance that Israel had the right to assert jurisdiction over offenses committed in Germany. Moreover, the
Supreme Court of Israel claimed this jurisdiction, not on the
ground that Israel was the legal representative of Eichmann's victims, but on the ground of universal jurisdiction over crimes
against humanity. Eichmann's crimes against non-Jewish Gypsies, Poles, and others were thus also germane to the proceedings
in Israel.[12]

In the Pinochet case, Lord Phillips of Worth Matravers discussed the question of universal jurisdiction and concluded:

> I believe that it is still an open question whether
> international law recognises universal jurisdiction in
> respect of international crimes—that is the right, under
> international law, of the courts of any state to prosecute for
> such crimes wherever they occur. In relation to war crimes,
> such a jurisdiction has been asserted by the State of Israel,
> notably in the prosecution of Adolf Eichmann, but this
> assertion of jurisdiction does not reflect any general state
> practice in relation to international crimes. Rather, states

have tended to agree, or to attempt to agree, on the creation of international tribunals to try international crimes. They have however, on occasion, agreed by conventions, that their national courts should enjoy jurisdiction to prosecute for a particular category of international crime wherever occurring.[13]

Belgium has legislation recognizing the principle of universal jurisdiction, and that legislation was invoked in the trial of four citizens of Rwanda on charges relating to their involvement in the 1994 genocide in that country. In June 2001, a Belgian jury found them guilty. In the same year, the President of Senegal agreed to a request from United Nations Secretary-General Kofi Annan to hold Hissène Habré, the former dictator of Chad, who is accused of presiding over a regime that carried out systematic torture and murdered 40,000 suspected political opponents. After complaints were filed in Belgian courts against Habré by relatives of his victims, Belgian judicial officials visited Chad in February 2002 to investigate whether the case against him is strong enough to support an application for his extradition to Belgium.[14]

In January 2001, at the initiative of the International Commission of Jurists, an international group of 30 scholars and jurists meeting at Princeton University attempted to reach consensus on a desirable direction for universal jurisdiction. They came very close: the "Princeton Principles on Universal Jurisdiction" were agreed to with only a single dissent among those assembled. The principles endorse the idea of criminal jurisdiction exercised by any state "based solely on the nature of the crime, without regard to where the crime was committed, the nationality of the alleged or convicted perpetrator, the nationality of the victim, or any other connection to the state exercising such jurisdiction." The crimes specified include piracy, slavery, war crimes, crimes against peace, crimes against humanity, genocide, and torture. Subsequent principles require adherence to international norms of due process, reject the idea of immunity for those in official positions such as head of state, and deny the efficacy of a grant of amnesty by a state to the accused.[15] If the Princeton Principles gain broad support internationally they would establish a truly global jurisdiction for the crimes they cover.

Yet it would be a mistake to disregard the reasons why the lone dissenter at the Princeton meeting, Lord Browne-Wilkinson, did not join the consensus. Like Lord Phillips of Worth Matravers, Lord Browne-Wilkinson is a distinguished judge of Britain's highest court, the House of Lords. He was the senior judge in the Pinochet case. In his dissenting statement, Lord Browne-Wilkinson warns that universal jurisdiction could lead to states hostile to other states seizing their officials and staging show trials for alleged international crimes. As examples he suggests—and this was written before September 11, 2001—that states hostile to the Western powers might put Western officials on trial, or Western zealots might seek to prosecute Islamic extremists for terrorist activities. The state of which the accused is a citizen might then resort to force in order to protect its subjects. The result "would be more likely to damage than to advance chances of international peace."[16]

In the same month (July 2001) in which the Princeton Principles were published, the fears that Lord Browne-Wilkinson had expressed came a step closer to reality. Ironically, in view of the role that the Eichmann case has played in establishing the principle of universal jurisprudence, this time it was Israel's Foreign Ministry that feared that Israeli officials might be put in the dock. The Foreign Ministry cautioned officials to take care in traveling abroad because some countries might be prepared to charge them with violating Palestinians' human rights. The warning followed a legal case brought in Belgium by survivors of the 1982 massacre of Palestinians at the Sabra and Shatila refugee camps against Israel's Prime Minister Ariel Sharon. Though Israel's Lebanese Christian allies carried out the massacre, an official Israeli investigation attributed "indirect responsibility" to Sharon, then defense minister, for failing to stop the killing. In Denmark there was also talk of arresting the Israeli ambassador, Carmi Gillon, a former chief of the Israeli security service, who had supported the use of "moderate physical pressure" during police investigations of suspected terrorists.[17] The ground for such cases was undercut, however, by a February 2002 ruling of the International Court of Justice that a Belgian arrest warrant for the acting Foreign Minister of the Democratic Republic of the Congo on charges of human rights violations was itself a violation of international law, because a foreign minister has immunity from such prosecutions. The court did not rule on the issue of universal jurisdiction itself, although remarks made by different judges suggested that the court would have been divided on the issue, had it directly addressed it.[18] (In accordance with standard diplomatic practice, the Princeton Principles provide immunity for diplomats and officials traveling on government business.)

To reduce the risk of a proliferation of charges brought by individual nations invoking universal jurisdiction, both Lord Browne-Wilkinson and his colleague Lord Phillips prefer the use of international courts, unless the country whose national has been charged has signed a treaty accepting universal jurisdiction for the relevant offenses, as in the case of Chile, which had signed the Convention against Torture. Even those who support universal jurisdiction agree that an international court is a valuable additional option. If it worked well enough, it might make universal jurisdiction unnecessary. Like the Nuremberg Tribunal, more recent international tribunals have arisen in the wake of tragic events: the wars that followed the break-up of the former Yugoslavia, the massacre of Hutus in Rwanda, the Serbian attacks on the Albanian inhabitants of Kosovo, and the killings in East Timor by militia supported by the Indonesian armed forces. By strengthening the resolve of all decent people not to allow such tragedies to continue, these tribunals are pushing us toward a global system of criminal justice for such crimes. In contrast to the Nuremberg Tribunal, the trial of Slobodan Milosevic, the former president of Yugoslavia, sent by the government he once led to trial by the international tribunal in The Hague, is not justice exacted by the occupying forces against the leaders of a nation that has been forced into unconditional surrender. It is a sign of the recognition, at least within Europe, that national sovereignty is no defense against a charge of crimes against humanity.

So far, these international tribunals have been one-time arrangements, specially set up to try particular crimes. (The long-standing International Court of Justice deals only with disputes between states, not with accusations against individuals.) To make the prosecution of crimes against humanity a permanent feature of international law, representatives of 160 states met in Rome in 1998 and agreed, by an overwhelming majority, to set up an International Criminal Court, to be associated with the United Nations and situated in The Hague. The court has a prosecutor who can bring charges of genocide, crimes against humanity, and war crimes against individuals as long as they are a national of a state that has ratified the treaty, or the crime was committed on the territory of such a state, or the Security Council refers a specific case to the court. The court came into existence in 2002, with more than 60 states accepting its jurisdiction and others acceding subsequently. Thus the world has, for the first time, a permanent international body enforcing international criminal law.

The United States has played a less than distinguished role in this process, seeking amendments to the statute that would exempt U.S. soldiers and government officials from prosecution. (Why the United States should expect its nationals to be treated differently from the nationals of all other nations has never been made clear.) President Clinton signed the treaty but did not attempt to have it ratified. President Bush has said that he is opposed to the court.[19] Conservative members of Congress are so hostile to the treaty that they held up the payment of money that the United States owed to the United Nations in an effort to obtain an exemption for U.S. officials or military personnel.[20] It is still too early to say whether American support for international prosecution of terrorists will, in time, lead to a change in the U.S. attitude to the International Criminal Court. If one country accuses another of harboring a terrorist, and the accused country is doubtful about whether the accused would receive a fair trial in the country making the charge, an international court is the obvious forum for resolving the dispute. (The treaty setting up the court does not give it authority to prosecute terrorists, because discussion of that issue became bogged down in disputes about how best to define "terrorism." There is, however, provision for further discussion of how best to frame a clause on prosecuting terrorism once the court has come into existence.) Although the United States refuses to contemplate its own citizens being tried by an open international court, operating in accordance with international rules of due process and eschewing the death penalty, it has, in the wake of the September 11, 2001 attacks, set up military tribunals for the trial of suspected terrorists who are not U.S. citizens, using evidence that need not be produced in open court. The tribunals will have the power to apply the death sentence.[21] Here again, as with the case of intellectual property rights over lifesaving medicines discussed in the previous chapter, the United

States uses one standard for its own citizens, and another for citizens of other countries.

Criteria for Humanitarian Intervention

Punishing the criminals after an atrocity has occurred is something that most people would support because of their belief that this is what justice requires. From a utilitarian perspective, punishing those guilty of past crimes will, one hopes, put others who might do something similar on notice that they will have no refuge from justice, and so deter them from committing new crimes. Since the fear of punishment will not always be sufficient to prevent the crimes taking place, however, the question of intervention will still arise. If punishment can be justified, so can intervention to stop a crime that is about to occur, or already in progress. Is there, perhaps, not only a right to intervene when atrocities are being committed, but, as a distinguished international commission suggested in the title of a report it presented in 2001, a "responsibility to protect" even if the only way to do so is to invade another country?[22] But if so, under what circumstances should countries act on that responsibility?

For philosophers to take up this question is not a new idea. Kant wrote a "philosophical sketch" entitled *Perpetual Peace* in which he argued that no state should, by force, interfere with the constitution or government of another state. He also thought that states preparing for war should seek the opinions of philosophers on the possibility of peace.[23] John Stuart Mill said that few questions are more in need of attention from philosophers than: when may a state that is not itself under attack go to war? He thought that philosophers should seek to establish "some rule or criterion whereby the justifiableness of intervening in the affairs of other countries, and (what is sometimes fully as questionable) the justifiableness of refraining from intervention, may be brought to a definite and rational test."[24]

What rule or criterion would satisfy Mill's "definite and rational test" of when intervention is justified, and even obligatory, and when it is not? One phrase often heard in this context is that used by Lassa Oppenheim in the following passage from his influential treatise on international law:

> There is general agreement that, by virtue of its personal and territorial supremacy, a State can treat its own nationals according to discretion. But there is a substantial body of opinion and practice in support of the view that there are limits to that discretion; when a state renders itself guilty of cruelties against and persecution of its nationals in such a way as to deny their fundamental rights *and to shock the conscience of mankind,* intervention in the interests of humanity is legally permissible.[25]

Michael Walzer has taken up this criterion. In *Just and Unjust Wars,* he wrote:

> Humanitarian intervention is justified when it is a response (with reasonable expectations of success) to acts "that shock the moral conscience of mankind." The old-fashioned language seems to me exactly right. . . . The reference is to the moral convictions of ordinary men and women, acquired in the course of their everyday activities. And given that one can make a persuasive argument in terms of those convictions, I don't think that there is any moral reason to adopt that posture of passivity that might be called waiting for the UN (waiting for the universal state, waiting for the messiah . . .).[26]

Those words date from 1977. Though the intervening years have not seen the arrival of the messiah, the United Nations has shown that it can act, even if its actions are open to serious criticism, and have not always been as prompt and effective as one would fervently wish.[27] Walzer has continued to support the "shock the conscience" criterion, and has pointed out that in an age in which "the camera crews arrive faster than rigor mortis," the acts that do shock the conscience of humankind are more shocking than they used to be, because we are so intimately linked to them.[28] Nevertheless, Walzer insists on retaining a strong presumption against intervention. He specifically rejects the idea that the violation of human rights is in itself a sufficient justification for intervention, or that it is legitimate to intervene for the sake of democracy.[29] Sometimes he argues for the strong presumption against intervention in terms of the importance of protecting the sovereignty of states in which people can live a communal life, and struggle for freedom in their own way, within their own communal structures.[30] At other times his argument is more pragmatic: ever since Roman times, he reminds us, imperial powers have sought to expand their empires by intervening in civil wars. Intervention can too easily become an excuse for annexation, in one form or another. Walzer does mention some examples of intervention that he thinks were justified: by India in what was then East Pakistan, now Bangladesh, in 1971; by Tanzania in 1979 against the regime of Idi Amin in Uganda; and by the Vietnamese in Cambodia in the same year. On the whole, though, he thinks people "should be allowed to work out their difficulties without imperial assistance, among themselves."[31]

The problem with Walzer's appeal to the "conscience of mankind" criterion is that this conscience has, at various times and places, been shocked by such things as interracial sex, atheism, and mixed bathing. Ironically, the Nazis themselves elevated "the healthy sensibility of the people" to the status of a legal norm, using it to suppress homosexuality.[32] We know that when international lawyers talk of acts that shock the conscience of humankind, they don't mean things like *that*, but how can we specify precisely what they do mean?

United Nations Secretary-General Kofi Annan has suggested that intervention is justified "when death and suffering are being inflicted on large numbers of people, and when the state nominally in charge is unable or unwilling to stop it." He defends this view by saying that the aim of the United Nations Charter is "to protect individual human beings, not to protect those who abuse them."[33] Annan's criterion has the advantage of being more specific than "shocking the conscience of mankind." In order to make it more precise still, however, the reference to "suffering" should be replaced by an enumeration of more specific harms. This is done in various international legal documents, including the 1948 Convention on the Prevention and Punishment of the Crime of Genocide, which is followed in the 1998 Rome Statute of the International Criminal Court. Article 2 of the Convention defines the crime of genocide as follows:

> genocide means any of the following acts committed with intent to destroy, in whole or in part, a national, ethnic, racial or religious group, as such:
> (a) Killing members of the group;
> (b) Causing serious bodily or mental harm to members of the group;
> (c) Deliberately inflicting on the group conditions of life calculated to bring about its physical destruction in whole or in part;
> (d) Imposing measures intended to prevent births within the group;

(e) Forcibly transferring children of the group to another group.[34]

Although all of these acts should count as crimes, and those who carry them out should be prosecuted and charged whenever possible, it is possible to draw distinctions between them. Since military intervention risks widespread casualties, the imposition of measures intended to prevent births within a group, or the forcible transfer of children from one group to another, is arguably insufficient in itself to justify military intervention. Of course, such measures will generally be accompanied by physical violence and can cause serious mental harm to members of the group, thus bringing the situation under one of the other clauses of the definition of genocide, and opening the way for the possible justification of intervention. In addition, whether the acts are carried out against a specific national, racial, ethnic, or religious group serves only to identify these crimes as genocide. Random acts of violence against an equivalent number of innocent people would be crimes against humanity, and they could also provide a trigger for justifiable intervention.

The definition of a "crime against humanity" is less well settled than the definition of genocide, but the Rome Statute of the International Criminal Court uses the following definition:

"crime against humanity" means any of the following acts when committed as part of a widespread or systematic attack directed against any civilian population, with knowledge of the attack:
(a) Murder;
(b) Extermination;
(c) Enslavement;
(d) Deportation or forcible transfer of population;

(e) Imprisonment or other severe deprivation of physical liberty in violation of fundamental rules of international law;

(f) Torture;

(g) Rape, sexual slavery, enforced prostitution, forced pregnancy, enforced sterilization, or any other form of sexual violence of comparable gravity;

(h) Persecution against any identifiable group or collectivity on political, racial, national, ethnic, cultural, religious, gender as defined in paragraph 3, or other grounds that are universally recognized as impermissible under international law, in connection with any act referred to in this paragraph or any crime within the jurisdiction of the Court;

(i) Enforced disappearance of persons;

(j) The crime of apartheid;

(k) Other inhumane acts of a similar character intentionally causing great suffering, or serious injury to body or to mental or physical health.[35]

Again, if we are seeking a trigger for military intervention, we need to focus on widespread, flagrant examples of these crimes.

We can now draw on the definitions of genocide and crimes against humanity, as well as Walzer's and Annan's criteria, to say:

Humanitarian intervention is justified when it is a response (with reasonable expectations of success) to acts that kill or inflict serious bodily or mental harm on large numbers of people, or deliberately inflict on them conditions of life calculated to bring about their physical destruction, and when the state nominally in charge is unable or unwilling to stop it.

Admittedly, this definition gives rise to more questions than it answers. How many people is a "large number"? How serious does the bodily or mental harm have to be? Who will decide when conditions of life that bring about the physical destruction of large numbers of people have been deliberately inflicted upon them? If humanitarian intervention is justified when this criterion is met, is there also an obligation on other nations to intervene? Could knowingly causing, or being unwilling to stop, environmental pollution that will kill large numbers of people be regarded as meeting the definition? Is it only things done to human beings that count? Might we one day see wiping out of tens of thousands of chimpanzees, or the destruction of a unique ecosystem, bringing with it the extinction of many species, as grounds for intervention?

These questions are difficult, perhaps too difficult to serve as the basis of political action for the foreseeable future. It is better to begin modestly, as the International Commission on Intervention and State Sovereignty set up by the Canadian government in 2000 did in its report *The Responsibility to Protect*. The commission, co-chaired by Gareth Evans, a former Foreign Minister of Australia, and Mohamed Sahnoun, an experienced Algerian diplomat, and consisting of twelve distinguished experts from as many different countries, was concerned that its recommendations should be politically feasible. To that end, the commission cut down the criteria for justifiable military action to just two:

> A. *large-scale loss of life,* actual or apprehended, with
> genocidal intent or not, which is the product either of
> deliberate state action, or state neglect or inability to act, or
> a failed state situation; or,
> B. *large-scale "ethnic cleansing,"* actual or apprehended,
> whether carried out by killing, forced expulsion, acts of
> terror or rape.

When these criteria are met, the commission said, there is not merely a right to intervene, but an international responsibility to protect those who are, or are in imminent danger of becoming, victims of these acts.[36]Although the conditions are in some respects narrower than those covered by the International Criminal Court's definition of a crime against humanity, and might therefore be thought to err on the side of making the threshold for intervention difficult to meet, in one important respect the commission's first criterion goes well beyond the definition of a crime against humanity: the "large-scale loss of life" that triggers intervention need not be the result of deliberate human action. Intervention can be justified, the commission said, to prevent people from starving to death, if the state is unable to assist them or neglects to do so.

These criteria seem, at least, a good starting point for the international community to use when it is considering a situation in which intervention is being considered. Let us therefore switch our attention to a different question: Who should decide when the criteria (whether it is precisely these, or some other set) have been satisfied? In practice, the answer to that question will be as important as the criteria. There is only one global body that could conceivably develop an authoritative procedure for specifying when intervention is justifiable.

The Authority of the United Nations

In a speech to the United Nations General Assembly in September 1999, Secretary-General Kofi Annan referred to the genocide in Rwanda as indicative of the consequences of inaction, and to the intervention in Kosovo as an example of action taken by "a regional organization [NATO] without a United Nations mandate." He then went on to pose a dilemma:

To those for whom the greatest threat to the future of international order is the use of force in the absence of a Security Council mandate, one might ask—not in the context of Kosovo but in the context of Rwanda: If, in those dark days and hours leading up to the genocide, a coalition of States had been prepared to act in defense of the Tutsi population, but did not receive prompt Council authorization, should such a coalition have stood aside and allowed the horror to unfold?

To those for whom the Kosovo action heralded a new era when States and groups of States can take military action outside the established mechanisms for enforcing international law, one might ask: Is there not a danger of such interventions undermining the imperfect, yet resilient, security system created after the Second World War, and of setting dangerous precedents for future interventions without a clear criterion to decide who might invoke these precedents, and in what circumstances?[37]

Annan made his own position clear, saying that state sovereignty is being redefined by the forces of globalization and international cooperation: "The State is now widely understood to be the servant of its people, and not vice versa." As we have seen, he reads the United Nations Charter as authorizing intervention to protect individual human beings, rather than those who abuse them. In saying this, Annan may have in mind Article 55(c) of the Charter, which refers to the promotion of "universal respect for, and observance of, human rights and fundamental freedoms for all," and Article 56, which reads: "All members pledge themselves to take joint and separate action in co-operation with the Organization for the achievement of the purposes set forth in Arti-

cle 55." The problem with interpreting these articles as justifying humanitarian intervention to protect individual human beings whose rights are being violated within a sovereign state, however, is that the same Charter states, in Article 2(7):

> Nothing contained in the present Charter shall authorize the United Nations to intervene in matters which are essentially within the domestic jurisdiction of any state or shall require the Members to submit such matters to settlement under the present Charter; but this principle shall not prejudice the application of enforcement measures under Chapter VII.

Chapter VII does not refer to human rights but only to "threats to the peace, breaches of the peace, and acts of aggression." If we take this at face value, it would seem that the United Nations cannot set up procedures to authorize humanitarian intervention, because in doing so, it would be violating its own Charter.

How can these different sections of the Charter be reconciled? The Charter places two sets of obligations on its members, to respect human rights and not to interfere in the internal matters of another state. As Brad Roth puts it: "the Organization and its Members are pledged to observe and promote, but bound not to impose, wholesome internal practices."[38] The "Declaration on Principles of International Law Concerning Friendly Relations and Co-Operation among States in Accordance with the Charter of the United Nations," adopted by the General Assembly in 1970 on the twenty-fifth anniversary of the United Nations, gives some support to this view. This Declaration elaborates on Article 2(7) of the Charter as follows:

> armed intervention and all other forms of interference or attempted threats against the personality of the State or

against its political, economic and cultural elements, are in violation of international law . . . Every state has an inalienable right to choose its political, economic, social and cultural systems, without interference in any form by another state.[39]

So does humanitarian intervention violate the United Nations Charter's acceptance of the principle of non-intervention in the domestic affairs of another sovereign state? We could reconcile the Charter with humanitarian intervention if we could defend at least one of the following claims:

1. That the violation of human rights, even in one country, is itself a threat to international peace.
2. That the existence of tyranny itself constitutes a threat to international peace.
3. That the rights of domestic jurisdiction retained by the states in Article 2(7) do not extend to committing crimes against humanity, nor to allowing them to be committed within one's domestic jurisdiction.

I shall discuss these claims in order.
1. The violation of human rights is itself a threat to international peace.

The first of these arguments is one that Annan himself has put forward. In referring to the United Nations Charter in his September 1999 speech, he said:

The sovereign States who drafted the Charter over half a century ago were dedicated to peace, but experienced in war.

They knew the terror of conflict, but knew equally that there are times when the use of force may be legitimate in the pursuit of peace. That is why the Charter's own words declare that "armed force shall not be used, save in the common interest." But what is that common interest? Who shall define it? Who will defend it? Under whose authority? And with what means of intervention? These are the monumental questions facing us as we enter the new century.

Taking these remarks in their context, Annan can be read as suggesting that the common interest should be defined so as to include an interest in preventing a tyrant from violating the rights of the citizens of the country over which he rules, even if the tyrant poses no threat to other nations. Though this may seem far-fetched, several decisions of the Security Council carry the same implication. In regard to Iraq, the Security Council resolved in 1991 that the repression of the civilian population, including that in Kurdish-populated areas, had consequences that were a threat to international peace and security. Since the Council mentioned the flow of refugees to other countries, it is arguable that this repression did have some consequences outside the borders of Iraq.[40] In authorizing intervention in Somalia, however, the Council simply determined that "the magnitude of the human tragedy caused by the conflict in Somalia, further exacerbated by the obstacles being created to the distribution of humanitarian assistance, constitutes a threat to international peace and security."[41] No further explanation was offered, and since the conflict was purely a civil one, it is not easy to guess how international peace would have been threatened if the Somalians had simply been left to starve, terrible as that would have been. Similarly, in Haiti the overthrow of the democratically elected president Jean-Bertrand Aristide was seen as a threat to "international peace and security in the region" and thus as justifying the use of Chapter VII powers.[42]

Given the human tragedies in Iraq, Somalia, and Haiti that the Security Council was trying to overcome, it is understandable that it should have been willing to stretch the language of its Charter to breaking point. It might seem that an ethic that looks to the consequences of our actions as determining what is right or wrong would lead us to support whatever stratagems offer the best prospect of preventing such tragedies. Taking a long-term view, however, a consequentialist should support the rule of international law because of its potential to reduce the likelihood of war. A consequentialist ethic may point to desirable changes in international law, but it will give it general support. Hence we should reject such blatant fictions as the idea that the overthrow of the president of Haiti is a threat to international peace. Once that is accepted, anything goes, and effectively the Security Council has an unconstrained mandate to interfere wherever it sees fit. There is no basis in international law for attributing such powers to the Security Council.

2. Democracies are the best guardians of peace.

A second strategy would be to invoke the argument that no war has ever occurred between two democratic states.[43] That thesis is controversial, and much depends on the definitions of "war" and of "democracy." If there has not yet been a counter-example, there no doubt will be one eventually. But the existence of one or two counter-examples does not refute a more cautiously stated version of the thesis, namely that democratic states are less likely to go to war with each other than are states that are not democracies. If this is the case, then it could be argued that Article 2 (7) no longer stands in the way of intervention for the sake of establishing or restoring democracy, since such interventions do reduce the general "threat to the peace" posed by non-democratic regimes. But should so vague and indefinite a threat to peace be sufficient reason for military intervention? Again, it seems that to do so is to use a pretext to cover intervention that is really motivated by another purpose altogether.

3. *The rights of domestic jurisdiction retained by the states in Article 2(7) do not extend to committing genocide or other crimes against humanity, nor to allowing them to be committed.*

The third strategy draws on the body of international law that, as suggested by the Eichmann case, holds that there is universal jurisdiction over those who commit genocide or other crimes against humanity. It asserts that the United Nations Charter cannot have intended, in granting domestic jurisdiction to the states, to set aside this important doctrine of customary international law.

One problem with interpreting the acceptance of domestic sovereignty in the United Nations Charter as limited by international law recognizing the crime of genocide and crimes against humanity is that the International Law Commission did not recommend that there should be international criminal responsibility for crimes against humanity until 1954, long after the Charter had been written and accepted by the original member states of the United Nations. Thus the Charter could well have been formulated and signed in the absence of any such belief. Nor do all nations, even today, accept limits to sovereignty. In July 2001, Russia and China signed a "Treaty on Good Neighborly Friendship and Cooperation" that appeared to interpret domestic sovereignty as providing immunity against intervention. Article XI of the treaty reads:

> The agreeing sides uphold the strict observance of
> generally recognized principles and norms of international
> law against any actions aimed at exerting pressure or
> interfering, under any pretext, with the internal affairs of
> the sovereign states and will make active efforts in order to

strengthen world peace, stability, development and cooperation.[44]

Despite these doubts, taking the view that domestic jurisdiction, as accepted in the United Nations Charter, does not extend to committing or allowing to be committed acts of genocide or crimes against humanity is the most plausible and promising of the three strategies so far considered. The International Commission on Intervention and State Sovereignty reached a similar conclusion, arguing that state sovereignty implies that the state has a responsibility for the protection of its people. When a state is unwilling or unable to fulfill that responsibility, the commission held, the responsibility falls upon the international community, and more specifically, on the Security Council, which under Article 24 of the United Nations Charter, has "primary responsibility for the maintenance of international peace and security." [45]

Unlike the first strategy, asserting that the violation of human rights is itself a threat to international peace, this third approach does not rely on a fiction, and unlike the second strategy, it does not rest on an unproven theory about the link between democracy and peace. Moreover it has built-in limits to the grounds on which intervention make take place. It may therefore be what we need. Nevertheless, before settling on the claim about the limits of domestic jurisdiction as the best justification for humanitarian intervention, I shall briefly mention a fourth, less obvious but more far-reaching strategy for reconciling humanitarian intervention with the principle of non-intervention in the domestic affairs of another sovereign state.

This fourth strategy builds on the discussion in the previous chapter questioning the standard view of what it takes for a government to be legitimate. As we saw there, although governments are generally accepted as legitimate if they have effective control over the territory they claim to rule, there is an alternative democratic view of legitimacy, according to which a regime that seizes power by force is not legitimate unless it gains from the people it rules a freely expressed indication of popular support. As we have seen, this democratic view can be defended both in terms of an argument from the right to self-government, and in consequentialist terms. If the democratic view were accepted, then the proposals made in the previous chapter in the context of trading restrictions might have a more far-reaching application. For if a government that came to power by force of arms and remained in power through the repression of all opposition was in virtue of that fact not to be considered a legitimate government, then it could not take its place at the United Nations. Hence if it were engaging in widespread violence against its own population, the provisions of the United Nations Charter restraining member nations against intervening in the internal affairs of other members would not apply. Though this doctrine could lead to an increase in war, this risk must be weighed against the prospect of supporting democracy and reducing the number of governments that are little more than gangs of brigands pillaging a country over which their guns hold sway. Of course, the usual consequentialist argument against going to war will still apply. War causes immense suffering and loss of life, and should always be a last resort, entered into when there is no other way of preventing still greater suffering and loss of life, and the prospects of success are good.

Will the Spread of Democracy Provide Protection Against Genocide?

In the first section of this chapter, I argued that there might be a genetic basis for the willingness of some human beings to massacre those who are not part of their group. Now I have suggested that where a regime rules by force, rather than in a democratic way, there is no legitimate sovereign to stand in the way of an intervention that can reasonably be expected to have good consequences—and presumably will, if possible, set up a democratic form of government. But, it may be objected, how can we have any faith in democracy as a means of preventing, rather than promoting, genocide? If the genes of violence are in many of us, why are they less likely to be in democratically elected rulers than in dictators?[46]

The worst genocides of this century have been carried out by governments that were very far from being democracies: Ottoman Turkey at the time of the Armenian genocide, Nazi Germany, the Soviet Union under Stalin, Cambodia under the Khmer Rouge. But Rwanda was moving toward a multi-party democracy at the time of the massacres, and since 85 percent of the population was Hutu, it is possible that more democracy would not have stopped the massacres of the Tutsis. An even more difficult counter-example for the view I am defending, however, is the government of Slobodan Milosevic, which bears substantial responsibility for the massacres in Bosnia and Kosovo. Milosevic was twice elected President of Serbia by large majorities, and later of Yugoslavia as well. Although neither Serbia nor Yugoslavia during this period was an entirely free and open society, to raise the bar for acceptance of a state as democratic so high as to exclude them would have the result that very many other putatively democratic states would also be excluded.[47]

Democracy, in the sense of the rule of the majority, does not provide a guarantee that human rights will be respected. But a democratic process requires that the policies of the government must be publicly defended and justified. They cannot simply be implemented from above. Although some of us may have the capacity to commit terrible crimes, many of us also have a moral sense, that is, a capacity to reflect on the rights and wrongs of what we are doing, or what our rulers are doing. That capacity emerges in the public arena. A small group may plot genocide, and inspire or terrify their followers to carry it out, but if genocide has to be defended on primetime television, it will become rare indeed. Even when the Nazis had been in power for eight years, ruling without opposition and making use of all the means of propaganda that Goebbels could devise, they did not dare to be open about what they were doing to the Jews. Himmler told a group of SS leaders that their work in exterminating the Jews was "an unwritten, never-to be written, glorious page of our history."[48] If it had been possible to ensure that every page of Nazi history were written as it happened, and offered for discussion to the German people, it is hard to believe that the Holocaust would have taken place. When the prosecutors at the Nuremberg Tribunal screened a film of Nazi concentration camps made by Allied military photographers, some of the defendants appeared visibly shocked. Even they may not have grasped exactly what the results of their policies looked like, close-up. Open procedures and public scrutiny may not be a perfect bulwark against genocide, but they do help.

Does Intervention Do More Good Than Harm?

The democratic concept of legitimate government implies that the concept of national sovereignty carries no weight if the government rests on force alone. It would seem that intervention in countries with such governments would then be readily justified. But if intervention is so easy to justify, will it not be used so often that it will be abused?

This objection rests on a failure to distinguish between legal and ethical justification. Even if intervention against a tyrannical regime that commits crimes against humanity violates neither international law nor the United Nations Charter, it might still be wrong to intervene. As Michael Doyle puts it, "it makes no moral sense to rescue a village and start World War Three, or destroy a village in order to save it."[49] We need to have rules and procedures making intervention difficult to justify, for as I have already noted, some nations are capable of deceiving themselves into believing that their desire to expand their influence in the world is really an altruistic concern to defend democracy and human rights. But even when those rules and procedures have been satisfied, the key question must always be: Will intervention do more good that harm?

Tzvetan Todorov has suggested that tyranny is not the greatest evil: anarchy is. Pointing to the downfall of the former communist regimes of Eastern Europe, he says that in some cases the collapse of the nation-state has led to a situation in which power is wielded by armed criminals. Intervention, even from humanitarian motives, can lead to the same outcome, because it too destroys the nation-state.[50] To the extent that this claim is factually correct, intervention should not take place.

There is an important ethical point at issue here, one that often leads to misguided objections to arguments about when it is right to intervene in the domestic affairs of another state. The objection runs: if it was justifiable to intervene against Serbia in Kosovo, then it must also be justifiable to intervene against Russia in Chechnya, or against China in Tibet. What this objection overlooks is that it is one thing for there to be a legal basis, and even a just cause, for intervening, and a totally different thing for intervention to be justified, all things considered. This distinction shows that the reason why NATO would have been wrong to intervene against Russia in Chechnya or against China in Tibet is not that (at least on one version of what the larger state is doing to the smaller one) there was no legal basis or just cause to intervene, but that the predictable human costs of the resulting war made it wrong to intervene. This should not be thought of as a case of "double standards." There is only one standard, that it is right to do what will have the best consequences, and that standard tells us not to intervene when the costs of doing so are likely to be greater than the benefits achieved.

Avoiding Cultural Imperialism

It is sometimes said that to intervene in other countries to protect human rights is a form of cultural imperialism. By what right, those who take this view ask, do we in the West impose on other peoples our view of the kind of society that they should have? Are we not repeating the errors of the Western missionaries who sailed out to Africa, or the South Sea Islands, and told the "primitive" people they found there to cover their nakedness, to practice monogamy, and to have sex only when prone, with the man on top? Have we not learned from this experience that morality is relative to one's own society, and our morals are no better than theirs?

This objection is confused. Moral relativists imagine that they are defending the rights of peoples of non-Western cultures to preserve their own values, but when moral relativism is taken seriously, it undermines all ethical arguments against cultural imperialism. For if morality is always relative to one's own society, then you, coming from your society, have your moral standards and I, coming from my society, have mine. It follows that when I criticize your moral standards, I am simply expressing the morality of my society, but it also follows that when you condemn me for criticizing the moral standards of your society, you are simply expressing the morality of your society. There is, on this view, no way of moving outside the morality of one's own society and ex-

pressing a transcultural or objective moral judgment about anything, including respect for the cultures of different peoples.
Hence if we happen to live in a culture that honors those who
subdue other societies and suppress their cultures—and the very
same people who defend moral relativism are often heard to assert that this *is* the Western tradition—then that is our morality,
and the relativist can offer no cogent reason why we should not
simply get on with it.

We should reject moral relativism. A much better case against
cultural imperialism can be made from the standpoint of a view
of ethics that allows for the possibility of moral argument beyond
the boundaries of one's own culture. Then we can argue that distinctive cultures embody ways of living that have been developed
over countless generations, that when they are destroyed the accumulated wisdom that they represent is lost, and that we are all
enriched by being able to observe and appreciate a diversity of
cultures. We can recognize that Western culture has no monop-
oly on wisdom, has often learned from other cultures, and still
has much to learn. We can urge sensitivity to the values of other
people, and understanding for what gives them self-respect and a
sense of identity. On that basis we can criticize the nineteenth-
century missionaries for their insensitivity to cultural differences,
and for their obsession with sexual behavior, an area in which human relationships take a wide variety of forms without any one
pattern being clearly superior to others. We can also argue that we
should be doing much more to preserve diverse cultures, especially indigenous cultures that are in danger of disappearing. But
once we accept that there is scope for rational argument in ethics,
independent of any particular culture, we can also ask whether
the values we are upholding are sound, defensible, and justifiable.
Although reasonable people can disagree about many areas of
ethics, and culture plays a role in these differences, sometimes

what people claim to be a distinctive cultural practice really serves the interests of only a small minority of the population, rather than the people as a whole. Or perhaps it harms the interests of some without being beneficial to any, and has survived because it is associated with a religious doctrine or practice that is resistant to change. Acts of the kind carried out by Nazi Germany against Jews, Gypsies, and homosexuals, by the Khmer Rouge against Cambodians they considered to be their class enemies, by Hutus against Tutsis in Rwanda, and by cultures that practice female genital mutilation or forbid the education of women are not elements of a distinctive culture that is worth preserving, and it is not imperialist to say that they lack the element of consideration for others that is required of any justifiable ethic.[51]

Some aspects of ethics can fairly be claimed to be universal, or very nearly so. Reciprocity, at least, seems to be common to ethical systems everywhere.[52] The notion of reciprocity may have served as the basis for the "Golden Rule"—treat others as you would like them to treat you—which elevates the idea of reciprocity into a distinct principle not necessarily related to how someone actually has treated you in the past. The Golden Rule can be found, in differing formulations, in a wide variety of cultures and religious teachings, including, in roughly chronological order, those of Zoroaster, Confucius, Mahavira (the founder of Jainism), the Buddha, the Hindu epic *Mahabharata,* the *Book of Leviticus,* Hillel, Jesus, Mohammed, Kant, and many others.[53] Over the past decade there has even been an attempt to draw up a "Declaration of a Global Ethic," a statement of principles that are universally accepted across all cultures. This project began with a meeting known as the "Parliament of the World's Religions"— more strictly, the Second Parliament of the World's Religions, for this one was held in Chicago in 1993, just a century after the first such parliament met. Different versions of the declaration are currently in circulation. One version, drafted by the theologian Hans Küng and approved at the Second Parliament of the World's Religions, begins with a fundamental demand that "every human being must be treated humanely." In making this demand more precise, it refers to the Golden Rule as "the irrevocable, unconditional norm for all areas of life." Leonard Swidler, who heads the Center for Global Ethics at Temple University in Philadelphia, has published a revised version that makes the Golden Rule itself the fundamental rule of ethics.[54]

The terrorist attacks of September 2001 appeared to constitute a breach in the idea of common cross-cultural ethical standards, for they suggested that it was consistent with Islamic teachings, and perhaps even a duty, to kill "infidel" civilians of nations that were seen as a threat to Islam. The overwhelming majority of Islamic clerics and scholars, however, repudiate this view. Though the attacks, and the support they evoked among some radical Moslems, suggest that agreement even on the prohibition of intentionally killing civilians is not entirely universal, it is very nearly so. So the search for an ethic that is global in the sense of drawing on aspects of ethics common to all or virtually all human societies could still meet with success. (It would, of course, be easier to agree on common ethical principles if we could first agree on questions that are not ethical but factual, such as whether there is a god, or gods, and if there is, or are, whether he, she, or they has or have expressed his, her, or their will or wills in any of the various texts claimed by the adherents of different religions to be divinely inspired. Unfortunately, on these matters we seem to be even further from agreement than we are on basic ethical principles.) If we are to achieve consensus on a common ethic, we are unlikely to be able to go beyond a few very broad principles. Hence, it may be said, these universally accepted ethical standards, if they exist at all, will not be the kind of thing that political leaders can draw on to show that they are justified in intervening in the affairs of another state.

Consider, for example, a nation with a conservative, devoutly religious population that supports a hereditary monarch ruling in accordance with the laws of the dominant religion. Suppose that the citizens support the Golden Rule, since their religion endorses it, but are opposed to the idea of democracy. On what grounds can others tell them that their nation should become a democracy?

The first point to make here is one that has already been mentioned. That a regime is not democratic does not mean that any form of intervention should take place. If the regime is not engaging in genocide or other crimes against humanity, the question of intervention does not arise. It is reasonable to distinguish between rulers exercising traditional authority and those that gain and hold power by military supremacy and repressive measures. Second, however, if the people living under hereditary monarchies prefer their form of government to a democracy, that preference ought to be testable. Hence it is possible to envisage a country choosing, at a free and open referendum, not to have elections for political office. This could then itself be seen as giving legitimacy to the non-democratic regime.

Nevertheless, the ultimate question of the relationship between democracy and sovereignty has not been solved. What if the monarchy, though expressing confidence that its people support it, does not wish to hold a referendum on its own existence? How can we give reasons, independent of our culture, for the view that legitimacy requires popular support, rather than resting on, say, religious law? Attempts to argue for the separation of church and state will not work, since that begs the question against the defenders of the religion that rejects such a separation. In the end, the challenge cannot be met without confronting the basis for belief in the religion. But one cannot argue that the religious faith of people of a different culture is false, while upholding a religious faith of one's own that rests on no firmer ground. That really would be cultural imperialism. In the end, at least as far as we are concerned with practices based on propositions about the existence of a god or gods and the authenticity of what are claimed to be divinely inspired scriptures, it is our capacity to reason that is the universal solvent. But this is not a question into which we can go further here.

Reforming the United Nations

I have urged that the United Nations should, within the limits of its capacities, authorize intervention to stop crimes against humanity, where it can reasonably expect to do so without doing greater harm than it prevents. This suggests not only a right to intervene, but in appropriate circumstances, a duty to intervene. To be able to do so, the United Nations needs to be able to draw on sufficient military force to make intervention effective. Ideally, the United Nations would have sufficient revenue to have its own military forces available for that purpose to defend civilians anywhere in the world threatened with genocide or large-scale crimes against humanity.

I have also suggested that there are reasons for moving toward a democratic idea of sovereignty, which would make it easier to justify intervention against a government that was not even minimally democratic. The combination of these two suggestions is not without its own irony: for the United Nations itself is scarcely a model of democracy. It was set up after the Second World War, and the Allies made sure that they retained firm control of it. This is most evident in the Security Council, which is the body that decides on matters of security, including whether to intervene in a dispute, either militarily or by means of sanctions. The Security

Council has five permanent members—the United States, the United Kingdom, France, China and Russia—corresponding to the major powers that were victorious in 1945. The General Assembly elects ten additional nations to the Security Council for two-year terms, but no substantive decision can be taken against the overt opposition of any of the five permanent members. The veto power of the permanent members, which was frequently used by both the Soviet Union and the United States during the cold war era, explains why during the 1960s and 1970s the Security Council effectively ignored the dominant conflict of the era, the Vietnam War.

There can be no justification today for giving special status to states that were great powers in 1945, but are no longer so today. Why should France or the United Kingdom have veto rights, and not Germany, or for that matter, Brazil? Why should China be a permanent member, and not India or Japan? Why should four of the five permanent members be European states, or states of European origin, when there is no permanent member from Africa, or Latin America or Southern or Southeastern Asia, or from anywhere in the Southern hemisphere? Is it desirable, if indeed we are facing a possible "clash of civilizations," that four of the five permanent members are states with roots in Christianity, and none of them is an Islamic state?[55]

What then should be done? To expand the number of permanent members with veto rights risks making the Security Council unworkable. A better idea would be to replace the veto with a requirement that substantive decisions be made by a special majority, two-thirds or three-quarters, of a reconstituted Security Council. To this it may be objected that the existing Security Council works reasonably well, and it is not clear that we would get a Council that worked better if we changed it to make it fairer. But if it is important and desirable to move toward greater global governance in a variety of areas—trade and the environment, for example, as well as peace and the protection of human rights— then the structure of the Security Council will make this difficult, because it is a constant reminder that the institutions of global governance are dominated by the wealthiest and most powerful states. In the long run, it is hard to see that giving special privileges to a small group of states will be the best way to maintain either the authority of the United Nations, or world peace.

A second objection to reform of the Security Council is simply that it is unthinkable, and would be perilous, for the Security Council to take military action against the implacable opposition of the United States or whatever other military superpower may in time emerge. Hence political realism requires allowing such superpowers a veto. This claim may be true; but if it is, the veto rights of the superpowers should be seen for what they are: the exercise of might, not right.

Compared to the Security Council, the General Assembly of the United Nations, which includes all 189 member states, seems more democratic. It is certainly not dominated by the same small circle of states that dominates the Security Council. The General Assembly, however, can take action only in very limited circumstances. Moreover its appearance of egalitarianism is misleading. It is an assembly of the world's states, not of the world's people. Some of the states are not themselves democratic, but even if we overlook this, there is the problem—as in the case of the WTO —that the government of India has the same voting power as the government of Iceland. In fact, if the 95 states with the smallest populations were to line up against the 94 states with the largest populations, it is possible that a General Assembly resolution could be supported by a majority of states that represented a combined total of only 198.5 million people, while on the other side, the outvoted 94 largest states would represent 5.7 billion. States representing less than 4 percent of the total United Nations member-state population could carry the day in the General Assembly.

There is an obvious solution to this problem, and it is not a new idea. At the end of the Second World War, when Britain's House of Commons debated the plan for a new United Nations, Ernest Bevin, the British Foreign Secretary, called for the "completion" of the United Nations design with "a world assembly elected directly from the people (to) whom the governments who form the United Nations are responsible."[56] In this respect the European Union, with its parliament directly elected by the people, could provide a model for a future, more democratic, United Nations. The European Parliament has, at present, only very limited powers. The plan is, however, for these to expand as the people and governments of Europe become comfortable with the parliament playing a larger role. There are, of course, major differences between the European Union and the United Nations. Most important to our present concerns is that, as we have seen, the European Union is in a position to set minimum standards for admission, including a democratic form of government and basic human rights guarantees. If the United Nations took a similar view, and ceased to recognize undemocratic governments as eligible for United Nations membership, it could then turn its General Assembly into a democratically elected World Assembly, as Bevin envisaged. But arguably, a United Nations that denied a voice to China, Saudi Arabia, and many other states would be less effective at maintaining world peace than one that was more inclusive.

A position halfway between the present system and one that excludes undemocratic governments is worth considering. The United Nations could remain open to all governments, irrespective of their form of government or observance of human rights, but it could replace the present General Assembly with a World

Assembly consisting of delegates allocated to its member states in proportion to their population. The United Nations would then supervise democratic elections, in every member country, to elect this delegation. A country that refused to allow the United Nations to supervise the election of its delegation would have only one delegate, irrespective of its population. That system would provide experience in democracy for the citizens of most countries, but would retain the inclusiveness that is an important feature of the United Nations.

Summing Up: National Sovereignty and a Global Ethic

A global ethic should not stop at, or give great significance to, national boundaries. National sovereignty has no *intrinsic* moral weight. What weight national sovereignty does have comes from the role that an international principle requiring respect for national sovereignty plays, in normal circumstances, in promoting peaceful relationships between states. It is a secondary principle, a rule of thumb that sums up the hard-won experience of many generations in avoiding war. Respect for international law is vital, but the international law regarding the limits of sovereignty is itself evolving in the direction of a stronger global community. As we have seen, the International Commission on Intervention and State Sovereignty has sought to reframe the debate in terms of "the responsibility to protect" rather than "the right to intervene." In doing so, the commission is suggesting that sovereignty is no longer simply a matter of the power of the state to control what happens within its borders. The limits of the state's ability and willingness to protect its people are also the limits of its sovereignty. The world has seen the horrific consequences of the failures of states like Cambodia, the former Yugoslavia, Somalia, Rwanda, and Indonesia to protect their citizens. There is now a broad consensus that, if it is at all possible to prevent such atrocities, they should be prevented. Only the United Nations should attempt to take on this responsibility to protect. Otherwise, national interests will again conflict and plunge the world into international conflict. If, however, the world's most powerful nations can accept the authority of the United Nations to be the "protector of last resort" of people whose states are flagrantly failing to protect them, and if those nations will also provide the United Nations with the means to fulfill this responsibility, the world will have taken a crucial step toward becoming a global ethical community.

5 one community

Human Equality: Theory and Practice

An "avalanche," a "flood"—these terms were used to describe the response to public appeals for the victims of the terrorist attacks of September 11, 2001. Three months after the disaster, the total stood at $1.3 billion. Of this amount, according to a *New York Times* survey, $353 million has been raised exclusively for the families of about 400 police officers, firefighters, and other uniformed personnel who died trying to save others. That comes to $880,000 for each family. The families of the firefighters killed would have been adequately provided for even if there had been no donations at all. Their spouses will receive New York state pensions equal to the lost salaries, and their children will be entitled to full scholarships to state universities. The federal government is giving an additional $250,000 to families of police officers and firefighters killed on duty.[1] For families to receive close to a million dollars in cash on top of all that may well leave us thinking that something has gone awry. But that was not all. Af-

ter initially being attacked for sensibly planning to reserve some
of the money for future needs, the American Red Cross went to
the opposite extreme and abandoned any attempt to examine
how much potential recipients needed help. It simply drew a line
across lower Manhattan, and offered anyone living below that
line the equivalent of three months' rent (or, if they owned their
own apartment, three months' mortgage and maintenance payments) plus money for utilities and groceries, if they claimed that
they had been affected by the destruction of the World Trade
Center. Most of the residents of the area below the line were not
displaced or evacuated, but they were offered mortgage or rent assistance nevertheless. One woman was told she could have the
cost of her psychiatric treatment reimbursed, even though she
said she had been seeing her psychiatrist before September 11. Red
Cross volunteers set up card tables in the lobbies of expensive
apartment buildings in Tribeca, where financial analysts, lawyers,
and rock stars live, to inform residents of the offer. The higher the
rent people paid, the more money they got. Some received as
much as $10,000. The Red Cross acknowledged that money was
going to people who did not need it. According to a spokesper-
son: "In a program of this sort, we're not going to make judgments on people's needs."[2]

As the terrorists were planning the attack, the United Nations
Children's Fund was getting ready to issue its 2002 report, *The
State of the World's Children*.[3] According to the UNICEF report,
released to the media on September 13, 2001, more than 10 million children under the age of five die each year from preventable
causes such as malnutrition, unsafe water, and the lack of even
the most basic health care. Since September 11, 2001 was probably
just another day for most of the world's desperately poor people,
we can expect that close to 30,000 children under five died from
these causes on that day—about ten times the number of victims

of the terrorist attacks. There was no "avalanche" of money for
UNICEF following the publication of these figures.

There are more than a billion people in the world living in dire
poverty. In the year 2000, Americans made private donations for
foreign aid of all kinds totaling about $4 per person in need, or
roughly $20 per family. New Yorkers, wealthy or not, living in
lower Manhattan on September 11, 2001, were able to receive an
average of $5,300 a family.[4] The distance between these amounts
symbolizes the way in which, for many people, the circle of concern for others stops at the boundaries of their own nation—if it
even extends that far. "Charity begins at home," people say, and
more explicitly, "we should take care of poverty in our own country before we tackle poverty abroad." They take it for granted that
national boundaries carry moral weight, and that it is worse to
leave one of our fellow citizens in need than to leave someone
from another country in that state. This is another aspect of the
attitudes described in Chapter 1. We put the interests of our fellow citizens far above those of citizens of other nations, whether
the reason for doing so is to avoid damaging the economic interests of Americans at the cost of bringing floods to the people of
Bangladesh, to avoid risking the lives of NATO troops at the cost
of more innocent lives in Kosovo, or to help those in need at
home rather than those in need abroad. While we do all these
things, most of us unquestioningly support declarations pro-
claiming that all humans have certain rights, and that all human
life is of equal worth. We condemn those who say the life of a person of a different race or nationality is of less account than the life
of a person of our own race or nation. Can we reconcile these attitudes? If those "at home" to whom we might give charity are already able to provide for their basic needs, and seem poor only
relative to our own high standard of living, is the fact that they are
our compatriots sufficient to give them priority over others with

greater needs? Asking these questions leads us to consider to what extent we really can, or should, make "one world" a moral standard that transcends the nation-state.

A Preference for Our Own

The popular view that we may, or even should, favor those "of our own kind" conceals a deep disagreement about who "our own kind" are. A century ago Henry Sidgwick, professor of moral philosophy at Cambridge University, described the moral outlook of his Victorian England as follows:

> We should all agree that each of us is bound to show kindness to his parents and spouse and children, and to other kinsmen in a less degree: and to those who have rendered services to him, and any others whom he may have admitted to his intimacy and called friends: and to neighbors and to fellow-countrymen more than others: and perhaps we may say to those of our own race more than to black or yellow men, and generally to human beings in proportion to their affinity to ourselves.[5]

When I read this list to students, they nod their heads in agreement at the various circles of moral concern Sidgwick mentions, until I get to the suggestion that we should give preference to our own race more than to "black or yellow men." At that point they sit up in shock.

Coming a little closer to our own time, we can find defenders of a much more extreme form of partiality:

> we must be honest, decent, loyal and friendly to members of our blood and to no one else. What happens to the Russians, what happens to the Czechs, is a matter of utter indifference to me. Such good blood of our own kind as

there may be among the nations we shall acquire for ourselves, if necessary by taking away the children and bringing them up among us. Whether the other races live in comfort or perish of hunger interests me only in so far as we need them as slaves for our culture; apart from that it does not interest me. Whether or not 10,000 Russian women collapse from exhaustion while digging a tank ditch interests me only in so far as the tank ditch is completed for Germany.[6]

That quotation is from a speech by Heinrich Himmler to SS leaders in Poland in 1943. Why do I quote such dreadful sentiments? Because there are many who think it self-evident that we have special obligations to those nearer to us, including our children, our spouses, lovers and friends, and our compatriots. Reflecting on what Sidgwick and Himmler have said about preference for one's own kind should subvert the belief that this kind of "self-evidence" is a sufficient ground for accepting a view as right. What is self-evident to some is not at all self-evident to others. Instead, we need another test of whether we have special obligations to those closer to us, such as our compatriots.

Ethics and Impartiality

How can we decide whether we have special obligations to "our own kind," and if so, who is "our own kind" in the relevant sense? Let us return for a moment to the countervailing ideal that there is some fundamental sense in which neither race nor nation determines the value of a human being's life and experiences. I would argue that this ideal rests on the element of impartiality that underlies the nature of the moral enterprise, as its most significant thinkers have come to understand it. The twentieth-century Oxford philosopher R. M. Hare argued that for judgments to count as moral judgments they must be universalizable, that is, the speaker must be prepared to prescribe that they be carried out in all real and hypothetical situations, not only those in which she benefits from them but also those in which she is among those who lose.[7] Consistently with Hare's approach, one way of deciding whether there are special duties to "our own kind" is to ask whether accepting the idea of having these special duties can itself be justified from an impartial perspective.

In proposing that special duties need justification from an impartial perspective, I am reviving a debate that goes back two hundred years to William Godwin, whose *Political Justice* shocked British society at the time of the French Revolution. In the book's most famous passage, Godwin imagined a situation in which a palace is on fire, and two people are trapped inside. One of them is a great benefactor of humanity—Godwin chose as his example Archbishop Fénelon, "at the moment when he was conceiving the project of his immortal *Telemachus.*" The other person trapped is the Archbishop's chambermaid. The choice of Fénelon seems odd today, since his "immortal" work is now unread except by scholars, but let's suppose we share Godwin's high opinion of Fénelon. Whom should we save? Godwin answers that we should save Fénelon, because by doing so, we would be helping thousands, those who have been cured of "error, vice and consequent unhappiness" by reading *Telemachus.* Then he goes on to make his most controversial claim:

> Supposing I had been myself the chambermaid, I ought to have chosen to die rather than that Fénelon should have died. The life of Fénelon was really preferable to that of the chambermaid. But understanding is the faculty that perceives the truth of this and similar propositions; and justice is the principle that regulates my conduct

accordingly. It would have been just in the chambermaid to have preferred the archbishop to herself. To have done otherwise would have been a breach of justice.

Supposing the chambermaid had been my wife, my mother or my benefactor. That would not alter the truth of the proposition. The life of Fénelon would still be more valuable than that of the chambermaid; and justice—pure, unadulterated justice—would still have preferred that which was most valuable. Justice would have taught me to save the life of Fénelon at the expense of the other. What magic is there in the pronoun "my" to overturn the decisions of everlasting truth? My wife or my mother may be a fool or a prostitute, malicious, lying or dishonest. If they be, of what consequence is it that they are mine?[8]

In 1971, at a time when several million Bengalis were on the edge of starvation, living in refugee camps in India so that they could escape from the massacres that the Pakistani army was carrying out in what was then East Pakistan, I used a different example to argue that we have an obligation to help strangers in distant lands. I asked the reader to imagine that on my way to give a lecture, I pass a shallow pond. As I do so, I see a small child fall into it and realize that she is in danger of drowning. I could easily wade in and pull her out, but that would get my shoes and trousers wet and muddy. I would need to go home and change, I'd have to cancel the lecture, and my shoes might never recover. Nevertheless, it would be grotesque to allow such minor considerations to outweigh the good of saving a child's life. Saving the child is what I ought to do, and if I walk on to the lecture, then no matter how clean, dry, and punctual I may be, I have done something seriously wrong.

Generalizing from this situation, I then argued that we are all, with respect to the Bengali refugees, in the same situation as the person who, at small cost, can save a child's life. For the vast majority of us living in the developed nations of the world have disposable income that we spend on frivolities and luxuries, things of no more importance to us than avoiding getting our shoes and trousers muddy. If we do this when people are in danger of dying of starvation and when there are agencies that can, with reasonable efficiency, turn our modest donations of money into life-saving food and basic medicines, how can we consider ourselves any better than the person who sees the child fall in the pond and walks on? Yet this was the situation at the time: the amount that had been given by the rich nations was less than a sixth of what was needed to sustain the refugees. Britain had given rather more than most countries, but it had still given only one-thirtieth as much as it was prepared to spend on the non-recoverable costs of building the Concorde supersonic jetliner.

I examined various possible differences that people might find between the two situations and argued that they were not sufficiently significant, in moral terms, to deflect the judgment that in failing to give to the Bengali refugees, we were doing something that was seriously wrong. In particular, I wrote:

> it makes no moral difference whether the person I help is a
> neighbor's child ten yards from me or a Bengali whose
> name I shall never know, ten thousand miles away.[9]

As far as I am aware, no one has disputed this claim in respect of distance per se—that is, the difference between ten yards and ten thousand miles. Of course, the degree of certainty that we can have that our assistance will get to the right person, and will really help that person, may be affected by distance, and that can make a difference to what we ought to do, but that is a different matter, and it will depend on the particular circumstances in which we find ourselves. What people *have* disputed, however, is that our obligation to help a stranger in another country is as great as the obligation to help one of our own neighbors or compatriots. Surely, they say, we have special obligations to our neighbors and fellow citizens—and to our family and friends—that we do not have to strangers in another country.[10]

Godwin faced similar objections. Samuel Parr, a well-known liberal clergyman of the time, preached and subsequently published a sermon that was a sustained critique of Godwin's "universal philanthropy."[11] As the text for his sermon, Parr takes an injunction from Paul's epistle to the Galatians, in which Paul offers yet another variant on who is "of our own kind": "As we have, therefore, opportunity, let us do good unto all men, especially unto them who are of the household of faith."[12] In Paul's words, Parr finds a Christian text that rejects equal concern for all, instead urging greater concern for those to whom we have a special connection. Parr defends Paul by arguing that to urge us to show impartial concern for all is to demand something that human beings cannot, in general and most of the time, give. "The moral obligations of men," he writes, "cannot be stretched beyond their physical powers."[13] Our real desires, our lasting and strongest passions, are not for the good of our species as a whole, but, at best, for the good of those who are close to us.

Modern critics of impartialism argue that an advocate of an impartial ethic would make a poor parent, lover, spouse, or friend, because the very idea of such personal relationships involves being partial toward the other person with whom one is in the relationship. This means giving more consideration to the interests of your child, lover, spouse, or friend than you give to a stranger, and from the standpoint of an impartial ethic this seems wrong. Feminist philosophers, in particular, tend to stress the importance of personal relationships, which they accuse male moral philosophers of neglecting. Nel Noddings, author of a book called *Caring*, limits our obligation to care to those with whom we can be in some kind of relationship. Hence, she states, we are "not obliged to care for starving children in Africa."[14]

Those who favor an impartial ethic have responded to these objections by denying that they are required to hold that we should be impartial in every aspect of our lives. Godwin himself wrote (in writing a memoir of Mary Wollstonecroft after her death following the birth of their first child):

> A sound morality requires that *nothing human should be regarded by us as indifferent;* but it is impossible we should not feel the strongest interest for those persons whom we know most intimately, and whose welfare and sympathies are united to our own. True wisdom will recommend to us individual attachments; for with them our minds are more thoroughly maintained in activity and life than they can be under the privation of them, and it is better that man should be a living being, than a stock or a stone. True virtue will sanction this recommendation; since it is the object of virtue to produce happiness; and since the man who lives in the midst of domestic relations will have many opportunities of conferring pleasure, minute in the detail, yet not trivial in the amount, without interfering with the purposes of general benevolence. Nay, by kindling his sensibility, and harmonising his soul, they may be expected, if he is endowed with a liberal and manly spirit, to render him more prompt in the service of strangers and the public.[15]

In the wake of his own grieving feelings for his beloved wife from whom he had been so tragically parted, Godwin found an impartial justification for partial affections. In our own times,

Hare's two-level version of utilitarianism leads to the same conclusion. Hare argues that in everyday life it will often be too difficult to work out the consequences of every decision we make, and
if we were to try to do so, we would risk getting it wrong because
of our personal involvement and the pressures of the situation. To
guide our everyday conduct we need a set of principles of which
we are aware without a lot of reflection. These principles form the
intuitive, or everyday, level of morality. In a calmer or more
philosophical moment, on the other hand, we can reflect on the
nature of our moral intuitions, and ask whether we have developed the right ones, that is, the ones that will lead to the greatest
good, impartially considered. When we engage in this reflection,
we are moving to the critical level of morality, that which informs
our thinking about what principles we should follow at the everyday level. Thus the critical level serves as a testing ground for
moral intuitions.[16] We can use it to test the list of special obligations suggested by the common moral sense of Victorian England as described by Henry Sidgwick: to parents, spouse, children, other kin, those who have rendered services to you, friends,
neighbors, fellow-countrymen, to "those of our own race . . . and
generally to human beings in proportion to their affinity to ourselves." Do any of these survive the demand for impartial justification, and if so, which ones?

Assessing Partial Preferences

The first set of preferences mentioned by Sidgwick—family,
friends, and those who have rendered services to us—stands up
quite well. The love of parents for their children and the desire of
parents to give preference to their children over the children of
strangers go very deep. It may be rooted in our nature as social
mammals with offspring who need our help during a long period
of dependence when they are not capable of fending for them-

selves. We can speculate that the children of parents who did not care for them would have been less likely to survive, and thus uncaring parents did not pass their genes on to future generations as frequently as caring parents did. Bonds between parents and children (and especially between mothers and children, for in earlier periods a baby not breast-fed by its mother was very unlikely to survive) are therefore found in all human cultures.

To say that a certain kind of behavior is universal and has its roots in our evolutionary history does not necessarily mean that it cannot be changed, nor does it mean that it should not be changed. Nevertheless in this particular case the experience of utopian social experiments has shown that the desire of parents to care for their children is highly resistant to change. In the early days of the Israeli kibbutzim the more radical of these socialist agricultural collectives sought to equalize the upbringing of children by having all children born to members of the kibbutz brought up communally, in a special children's house. For parents to show particular love and affection for their own child was frowned upon. Nevertheless, mothers used to sneak into the communal nursery at night to kiss and hold their sleeping children. Presumably, if they shared the ideals of the kibbutz, they felt guilty for doing so.[17]

So even if, like the founders of these collective settlements, we were to decide that it is undesirable for parents to favor their own children, we would find such favoritism very difficult to eradicate. Any attempt to do so would have high costs and would require constant supervision or coercion. Unless we are so intent on suppressing parental bias that we are willing to engage in an all-out campaign of intense moral pressure backed up with coercive measures and draconian sanctions, we are bound to find that most parents constantly favor their children in ways that cannot be directly justified on the basis of equal consideration of interests. If we were to engage in such a campaign, we may well bring about guilt and anxiety in parents who want to do things for their children that society now regards as wrong. Such guilt will itself be a source of much unhappiness. Will the gains arising from diminished partiality for one's own children outweigh this? That seems unlikely, because for the children themselves, the care of loving and partial parents is likely to be better than the care of impartial parents or impartial community-employed carers. There is evidence, too, that children are more likely to be abused when brought up by people who are not their biological parents.[18] Given the unavoidable constraints of human nature and the importance of bringing children up in loving homes, there is an impartial justification for approving of social practices that presuppose that parents will show some degree of partiality towards their own children.

It is even easier to find an impartial reason for accepting love and friendship. If loving relationships, and relationships of friendship, are necessarily partial, they are also, for most people, at the core of anything that can approximate to a good life. Very few human beings can live happy and fulfilled lives without being attached to particular other human beings. To suppress these partial affections would destroy something of great value, and therefore cannot be justified from an impartial perspective.

Bernard Williams has claimed that this defense of love and friendship demands "one thought too many."[19] We should, he says, visit our sick friend in hospital because he is our friend and is in hospital, not because we have calculated that visiting sick friends is a more efficient way of maximizing utility than anything else we could do with our time. This objection may have some force if pressed against those who claim that we should be thinking about the impartial justification of love or friendship at the time when we are deciding whether to visit our sick friend;

but it is precisely the point of two-level utilitarianism to explain why we *should* have an extra thought when we are thinking at the critical level, but not at the level of everyday moral decision-making.

Consider the idea, supported to various degrees in the passages I have quoted from Sidgwick and Himmler, to the effect that whites should care more for, and give priority to, the interests of other whites, or that "Aryans" should give priority to the interests of others "of their blood." These ideas have had, in their time, an intuitive appeal very similar to the intuitive appeal of the idea that we have obligations to favor family and friends. But racist views have contributed to many of the worst crimes of our century, and it is not easy to see that they have done much good, certainly not good that can compensate for the misery to which they have led. Moreover, although the suppression of racism is difficult, it is not impossible, as the existence of genuinely multiracial societies, and even the history of desegregation in the American South, shows. White people in the South no longer think twice about sharing a bus seat with an African American, and even those who fought to defend segregation have, by and large, come to accept that they were wrong. Taking an impartial perspective shows that partialism along racial lines is something that we can and should oppose, because our opposition can be effective in preventing great harm to innocent people.

Thus we can turn Williams' aphorism against him: philosophers who take his view have one thought too few. To be sure, to think *always* as a philosopher would mean that, in our roles as parent, spouse, lover and friend, we would indeed have one thought too many. But if we *are* philosophers, there should be times when we reflect critically on our intuitions—indeed not only philosophers, but all thoughtful people, should do this. If we were all simply to accept our feelings without the kind of extra reflection we have just been engaged in, we would not be able to decide which of our intuitive inclinations to endorse and support and which to oppose. As the quotations from Sidgwick and Himmler indicate, the fact that intuitive responses are widely held is not evidence that they are justified. They are not rational insights into a realm of moral truth. Some of them—roughly, those that we share with others of our species, irrespective of their cultural background—are responses that, for most of our evolutionary history, have been well suited to the survival and reproduction of beings like us. Other intuitive responses—roughly, those that we do not share with humans from different cultures —we have because of our particular cultural history. Neither the biological nor the cultural basis of our intuitive responses provides us with a sound reason for taking them as the basis of morality.

Let us return to the issue of partiality for family, lovers and friends. We have seen that there are impartial reasons for accepting some degree of partiality here. But how much? In broad terms, as much as is necessary to promote the goods mentioned above, but no more. Thus the partiality of parents for their children must extend to providing them with the necessities of life, and also their more important wants, and must allow them to feel loved and protected; but there is no requirement to satisfy every desire a child expresses, and many reasons why we should not do so. In a society like America, we should bring up our children to know that others are in much greater need, and to be aware of the possibility of helping them, if unnecessary spending is reduced. Our children should also learn to think critically about the forces that lead to high levels of consumption, and to be aware of the environmental costs of this way of living. With lovers and friends, something similar applies: the relationships require partiality, but they are stronger where there are shared values, or at least respect for the values that each holds. Where the values shared include concern for the welfare of others, irrespective of whether they are friends or strangers, then the partiality demanded by friendship or love will not be so great as to interfere in a serious way with the capacity for helping those in great need.

What of the other categories on Sidgwick's list of those to whom we are under a special obligation to show kindness: parents, kin, "those who have rendered services," "neighbors" and "fellow-countrymen"? Can all of these categories be justified from an impartial perspective? The inclusion of "those who have rendered services" is seen by ethicists who rely on intuition to be a straight-forward case of the obligation of gratitude.[20] From a two-level perspective, however, the intuition that we have a duty of grati-tude is not an insight into some independent moral truth, but something desirable because it helps to encourage reciprocity, which makes cooperation, and all its benefits, possible. As we saw in Chapter 4, here too, evolutionary theory can help us to see why reciprocity, and with it the sense of gratitude, should have evolved and why it is, in some form or other, a universal norm in all human societies.[21] (To give such an evolutionary explanation, however, says nothing about the motives people have when they engage in cooperative behavior, any more than explaining sexual behavior in terms of reproduction suggests that people are moti-vated to have sex because they wish to have children.)

Once a duty of gratitude is recognized, it is impossible to ex-clude parents from the circle of those to whom a special duty of kindness is owed. Because parents have generally rendered count-less services to their children, we can hardly subscribe to a general principle of gratitude without recognizing a duty of children to-ward their parents. The exception here would be children who have been maltreated or abandoned by their parents—and it is the exception that proves the rule, in the sense that it shows that the obligation is one of gratitude, not one based on blood relationships.

Another of Sidgwick's categories, that of our neighbors, can be handled in the same way. Geographical proximity is not in itself of any moral significance, but it may give us more opportunities to enter into relationships of friendship and mutually beneficial reciprocity. Of course, increasing mobility and communication have, over the course of the past century, eroded the extent to which neighbors are important to us. When we run out of sugar, we don't go next door to borrow some, because the supermarket down the street has plenty. We walk past our neighbors, barely nodding at them, as we talk on our cell phones to friends in other cities. In these circumstances it becomes doubtful if we have special duties of kindness to our neighbors at all, apart from, perhaps, a duty to do the things that only neighbors can do, such as feeding the cat when your neighbor goes on vacation.

"Kin," the next on Sidgwick's list, is an expression that ranges from the sibling with whom you played as a child and with whom you may later share the task of caring for your parents, to the distant cousin you have not heard from for decades. The extent to which we have a special obligation to our kin should vary accordingly. Kin networks can be important sources of love, friendship, and mutual support, and then they will generate impartially justifiable reasons for promoting these goods. But if that distant cousin you have not heard from for decades suddenly asks for a loan because she wants to buy a new house, is there an impartially defensible ground for believing that you are under a greater obligation to help her than you would be to help an unrelated equally distant acquaintance? At first glance, no, but perhaps a better answer is that it depends on whether there is a recognized system of cooperation among relatives. In rural areas of India, for example, such relationships between relatives can play an important role in providing assistance when needed, and thus in reducing harm when something goes awry.[22] Under these circumstances there is an impartial reason for recognizing and supporting this practice. In the absence of any such system, there is not. (In different cultures, the more impersonal insurance policy plays the same harm-reduction role, and thus reduces the need for a system of special obligations to kin, no doubt with both good and bad effects.)

The Ethical Significance of the Nation-State
Compatriots as Extended Kin

Finally, then, what impartial reasons can there be for favoring one's compatriots over foreigners? On some views of nationality, to be a member of the same nation is like an extended version of being kin. Michael Walzer expresses this view when, in discussing immigration policy, he writes:

> Clearly, citizens often believe themselves morally bound to open the doors of their country—not to anyone who wants to come in, perhaps, but to a particular group of outsiders, recognized as national or ethnic "relatives." In this sense, states are like families rather than clubs, for it is a feature of families that their members are morally connected to people they have not chosen, who live outside the household.[23]

Germany's former citizenship law embodied the sense of nationality that Walzer has in mind. Descendants of German farmers and craft workers who settled in Eastern Europe in the eighteenth century are recognized in the German Constitution as having the right to "return" to Germany and become citizens, although most of them do not speak German and come from families none of whom have set foot in the country for generations. On the other hand, before new citizenship laws came into effect in 2000, foreign guest workers could live in Germany for decades without becoming eligible for citizenship, and the same was true of their children, even though they were born in Germany, educated in German schools, and had never lived anywhere else. Although Germany's pre-2000 laws were an extreme case of racial or ethnic preference, most other nations have, for much of their history, used racist criteria to select immigrants, and thus citizens. As late as 1970, when immigrants of European descent were being actively encouraged to become Australian citizens, the "White Australia" policy prevented non-European immigrants from settling in Australia.

If we reject the idea that we should give preference to members of one's own race, or those "of our blood," it is difficult to defend the intuition that we should favor our fellow citizens, in the sense in which citizenship is seen as a kind of extended kinship, because all citizens are of the same ethnicity or race. The two are simply too close.

A Community of Reciprocity

What if we empty all racist elements from the idea of who our fellow citizens are? We might hold that we have a special obligation to our fellow citizens because we are all taking part in a collective enterprise of some sort. Eammon Callan has suggested that to be a citizen in a state is to be engaged in a community of reciprocity:

> So far as citizens come to think of justice as integral to a particular political community they care about, in which their own fulfillment and that of their fellow citizens are entwined in a common fate, the sacrifices and compromises that justice requires cannot be sheer loss in the pursuit of one's own good.[24]

Walter Feinberg takes a similar view:

> The source of national identity is . . . connected to a web
> of mutual aid that extends back in time and creates future
> obligations and expectations.[25]

The outpouring of help from Americans for the families of the
victims of September 11 was a striking instance of this web of mutual aid, based on the sense that Americans will help each other in
times of crisis. In more normal times, Americans can still feel that
by their taxes they are contributing to the provision of services
that benefit their fellow-Americans by providing social security
and medical care when they retire or become disabled, fight crime,
defend the nation from attack, protect the environment, maintain national parks, educate their children, and come to the rescue in case of floods, earthquakes or other natural disasters. If
they are male, and old enough, they may have served in the armed
forces in wartime, and if they are younger, they might have to do
so in the future.

It is therefore possible to see the obligation to assist one's fellow-
citizens ahead of citizens of other countries as an obligation of
reciprocity, though one that is attenuated by the size of the community and the lack of direct contact between, or even bare knowledge of, other members of the community. But is this sufficient
reason for favoring one's fellow citizens ahead of citizens of other
countries whose needs are far more pressing? Most citizens are
born into the nation, and many of them care little for the nation's
values and traditions. Some may reject them. Beyond the borders
of the rich nations are millions of refugees desperate for the opportunity to become part of those national communities. There
is no reason to think that, if we admitted them, they would be
any less ready than native-born citizens to reciprocate whatever

benefits they receive from the community. If we deny admission to these refugees, it hardly seems fair to then turn around and discriminate against them when we make decisions about whom we will aid, on the grounds that they are not members of our community and have no reciprocal relationships with us.

The Imagined Community

If reciprocity alone is not enough to show why we have a significantly stronger obligation to our fellow-citizens than to anyone else, one might try to supplement this idea by recourse to Benedict Anderson's account of a nation as an "imagined political community," one that lives only in the minds of those who see themselves as citizens of the same nation.[26] Though citizens never encounter most of the other members of the nation, they think of themselves as sharing an allegiance to common institutions and values, such as a constitution, democratic procedures, principles of toleration, the separation of church and state, and the rule of law. The imagined community makes up for the lack of a real, face-to-face community in which there would be personal ties and more concrete obligations of reciprocity. Acknowledging special obligations to other members of the nation can then be seen as part of what it takes to form and maintain this imagined community.

Anderson's conception of nationalism is an account of how the idea of belonging to a nation took hold in the modern world. Because it is a description and not a prescription, it cannot ground a moral argument for the importance of maintaining the imagined communities that he describes. It is nevertheless an illuminating account, precisely because it shows that the modern idea that we owe special loyalty to our national community is not based on a community that exists independently of the way we think about ourselves. If Anderson is right, and the modern idea of the nation rests on a community we imagine ourselves to be part of, rather than one that we really are part of, then it is also possible for us to imagine ourselves to be part of a different community. That fits well with the suggestion that the complex set of developments we refer to as globalization should lead us to reconsider the moral significance we currently place on national boundaries. We need to ask whether it will, in the long run, be better if we continue to live in the imagined communities we know as nation-states, or if we begin to consider ourselves as members of an imagined community of the world. I have already offered several arguments for the latter view. Our problems are now too intertwined to be well resolved in a system consisting of nation-states, in which citizens give their primary, and near-exclusive, loyalty to their own nation-state rather than to the larger global community, and such a system has not led to a great enough will to meet the pressing needs of those living in extreme poverty. Imagining ourselves to be part of a national community seems fine when we think of it as broadening our concerns beyond more limited tribal loyalties, but it is less appealing when we think of it as erecting fences against the rest of the world.

The Efficiency of Nations

Robert Goodin defends a system of special obligations to our compatriots "as an administrative device for discharging our general duties more efficiently."[27] If you are sick and in hospital, Goodin argues, it is best to have a particular doctor made responsible for your care, rather than leaving it up to all the hospital doctors in general; so too, he says, it is best to have one state that is clearly responsible for protecting and promoting the interests of every individual within its territory. There is no doubt something in this, but it is an argument with very limited application in the real world. In any case, efficiency in administration within units is one thing, and the distribution of resources between units is another. Goodin recognizes this, saying:

> If there has been a misallocation of some sort, so that some states have been assigned care of many more people than they have been assigned resources to care for them, then a reallocation is called for.[28]

While it may, other things being equal, be more efficient for states to look after their own citizens, this is not the case if wealth is so unequally distributed that a typical affluent couple in one country spends more on going to the theater than many in other countries have to live on for a full year. In these circumstances the argument from efficiency, understood in terms of gaining the maximum utility for each available dollar, far from being a defense of special duties toward our compatriots, provides grounds for holding that any such duties are overwhelmed by the much greater good that we can do abroad.

Justice Within States and Between States

Christopher Wellman has suggested three further impartial reasons for thinking that it may be particularly important to prevent economic inequality from becoming too great *within* a society, rather than *between* societies. The first is that political equality within a society may be adversely affected by economic inequality within a society, but is not adversely affected by economic inequality between societies. The second is that inequality is not something that is bad in itself, but rather something that is bad in so far as it leads to oppressive relationships, and hence we are right to be more concerned about inequality among people living in the same nation than we are about inequality between people living in different countries who are not in a meaningful relationship with each other. And the third is a point about the comparative nature of wealth and poverty.[29]

Wellman's first two points are at least partly answered by the phenomenon that underlies so much of the argument of this book: increasingly, we are facing issues that affect the entire planet. Whatever it is we value about political equality, including the opportunity to participate in the decisions that affect us, globalization means that we should value equality between societies, and at the global level, at least as much as we value political equality within one society. Globalization also means that there can be oppressive relationships at the global scale, as well as within a society.

Marx provided the classic formulation of Wellman's third point:

> A house may be large or small; as long as the surrounding houses are equally small it satisfies all social demands for a dwelling. But let a palace arise beside the little house, and it shrinks from a little house to a hut . . . however high it may shoot up in the course of civilization, if the neighboring palace grows to an equal or even greater extent, the occupant of the relatively small house will feel more and more uncomfortable, dissatisfied and cramped with its four walls.[30]

But today it is a mistake to think that people compare themselves only with their fellow citizens (or with all their fellow citizens). Inhabitants of rural Mississippi, for example, probably do not often compare themselves with New Yorkers, or at least not in regard to income. Their lifestyle is so different that income is merely one element in a whole package. On the other hand, many Mexicans obviously do look longingly north of the border, and think how much better off they would be financially if they could live in the United States. They reveal their thoughts by trying to get across the border. And the same can be true of people who are not in close geographical proximity, as we can see from the desperate attempts of Chinese to travel illegally to the United States, Europe, and Australia, not because they are being politically persecuted, but because they already have enough of an idea about life in those far-away countries to want to live there.

Despite the different picture that globalization gives, let us grant that there are some reasons for thinking that we should place a higher priority on avoiding marked economic inequality within a given society than across the entire range of the planet's inhabitants. Wellman's three points can be given some weight when they are brought against the strong claim that it is *no* less desirable to eliminate marked economic inequality between any of the world's inhabitants than it is to eliminate it within a single society. But the weight we should give them is limited, and subject to particular circumstances. In particular, the question of whether to seek greater equality within societies, or between societies only arises if we cannot do both. Sometimes we can. We can increase taxes on people in rich nations who have higher incomes or leave large sums to their heirs, and use the revenue to increase aid to those people in the world's poorest nations who have incomes well below average even for the nation in which they are living. That would reduce inequality both in the poor nations and between nations.

Granted, if we live in a rich nation, we could reduce equality within our own society even further if we used the revenue generated by taxes on the wealthiest people within our own society to help the worst-off within our own society. But even if we accept Wellman's arguments, that would be the wrong choice. For then we would be choosing to reduce inequality within our own nation rather than reducing both inequality within poor nations, and inequality between nations. Wellman has offered reasons why it may be more important to focus on inequality within a nation than on inequality between nations, but that is not the same as finding reasons for giving greater priority to overcoming inequality within one's *own* society than in any other society. If I, living in America, can do more to reduce inequality in, say, Bangladesh than I can do to reduce inequality my own country, then Wellman has not given me any grounds for preferring to reduce equality in America—and if giving money to those near the bottom of the economic ladder in Bangladesh will both reduce inequality there and reduce inequality between nations, that seems the best thing to do. Wellman has failed to find any magic in the pronoun "my."

In any case, in the present situation we have duties to foreigners that override duties to our fellow citizens. For even if inequality is often relative, the state of absolute poverty that has already been described is a state of poverty that is not relative to someone else's wealth. Reducing the number of human beings living in absolute poverty is surely a more urgent priority than reducing the relative poverty caused by some people living in palaces while others live in houses that are merely adequate. Here Sidgwick's account of the common moral consciousness of his time is in agreement. After giving the list of special obligations I quoted above, he continues:

> And to all men with whom we may be brought into
> relation we are held to owe slight services, and such as may
> be rendered without inconvenience: but those who are in
> distress or urgent need have a claim on us for special
> kindness.

Rawls and *The Law of Peoples*

I have already referred to the remarkable fact that the most influential work on justice written in twentieth-century America, John Rawls's *A Theory of Justice,* does not address the issue of justice between societies. With the more recent publication of *The Law of Peoples,* however, Rawls has at last addressed himself to the issue of justice beyond the borders of our own society. Rawls believes that well-off societies have significant obligations toward struggling societies, but there is a lack of focus on obligations toward individuals who are currently destitute in other countries. The book is, after all, called *The Law of Peoples,* not, for example, *A Theory of Global Justice.*

Here is one example of how the book Rawls has written differs from the book that he might have written. Rawls asks us to consider a world in which there are two societies, each of which satisfies internally the two principles of justice in *A Theory of Justice,* and in which the worst-off representative person in the first society is worse off than the worst-off representative person in the second. He then supposes that it is possible to arrange a global redistribution that would improve the lot of the worst-off representative person in the first society, while allowing both societies to continue to satisfy his two principles of justice internally. We are, in other words, being asked to consider two societies, each of which is just if we confine our gaze to its own boundaries, but one of which has people in it who are worse off than anyone in the other society. Should we prefer a redistribution that would lessen the gap between the worst-off people in the two societies? No, Rawls says, "The Law of Peoples is indifferent between the two distributions."[31]

In *A Theory of Justice* Rawls argues for a system of justice in which "no one is advantaged or disadvantaged in the choice of principles by the outcome of natural chance or the contingency of social circumstances."[32] Now, however, he declares his theory *indifferent* to the consequences of something as contingent as which side of a national border one happens to live. These two positions cannot be reconciled. In *The Law of Peoples* Rawls uses an approach quite different from that of *A Theory of Justice.* Though both books refer to an "original position," in the earlier work the deliberating parties in the original position weigh up alternative principles of justice, such as classical utilitarianism and moral perfectionism, and choose between them. In the "original position" of *The Law of Peoples,* on the other hand, the deliberating parties—whose task now is to decide on a framework for international relationships—do not even consider classical utilitarianism as a possible principle by which they might regulate the way in which peoples behave toward each other. This is because, Rawls tells us:

> a classical, or average, utilitarian principle would not be accepted by peoples, since no people organized by its government is prepared to count, *as a first principle,* the benefits for another people as outweighing the hardships imposed on itself.[33]

This claim, which looks like an odd anticipation of President Bush's "first things first are the people who live in America," is no doubt true, at the level of sociological description of peoples organized as governments in existing societies. But how does that justify Rawls in using it as a conclusive ground for ruling out of consideration any possibility that peoples *would* choose to accept this principle, if they were choosing in the original position, in which they did not know which society they would be living in?

Why should we regard what governments are *now* prepared to accept as decisive about what they *would* accept, if they were choosing impartially?

Another strange aspect of *The Law of Peoples* is Rawls's readiness to invoke, against the idea of economic redistribution between nations, arguments that could easily be brought—indeed have been brought—against economic redistribution between individuals or families *within* the same nation. Thus he invites us to consider an example of two countries that are at the same level of wealth and have the same size population. The first decides to industrialize, while the second prefers a more pastoral and leisurely society and does not. Decades later, the first is twice as wealthy as the second. Assuming that both societies freely made their own decisions, Rawls asks whether the industrializing society should be taxed to give funds to the pastoral one. That, he says, "seems unacceptable."[34] But if Rawls finds this unacceptable, how does he answer the critics of his position in *A Theory of Justice* who find it unacceptable for a person who has worked hard and achieved wealth to be taxed in order to support someone who has led a more relaxed life and so is now, in terms of resources held, among the worst-off members of society? Both cases raise a problem for anyone who supports the redistribution of wealth, and if the problem can be answered in the case of redistribution within a society, I see no reason why it cannot be answered in the case of redistribution between societies.

Rawls does urge in *The Law of Peoples* that "well-ordered peoples have a *duty* to assist burdened societies," that is, those societies that "lack the political and cultural traditions, the human capital and know-how, and, often, the material and technological resources needed to be well-ordered."[35] The duty extends only to the requirement of assistance to help the societies to become "well-ordered," by which Rawls means a society that is designed to advance the good of its members and is effectively regulated by a public conception of justice.[36] In considering what can help a society to become well-ordered, Rawls places emphasis on the need for societies to develop a suitable culture, for he conjectures "that there is no society anywhere in the world—except for marginal cases—with resources so scarce that it could not, were it reasonably and rationally organized and governed, become well-ordered."[37] This conjecture may or may not be correct, but the emphasis on the need for a change of culture leaves untouched the plight of individuals who are dying from starvation, malnutrition, or easily preventable diseases *right now*, in countries that presently lack the capacity to provide for the needs of all their citizens.

Rawls says, in the course of discussing contrary views of international justice advanced by Charles Beitz and Thomas Pogge, that he shares their goals "of attaining liberal or decent institutions, securing human rights and meeting basic needs," and he believes that these goals "are covered by the duty of assistance."[38] But if this means that wealthy societies have a duty of assistance to help individuals who are starving or otherwise unable to satisfy their "basic needs," it fails to receive the emphasis that it deserves. Instead Rawls writes of the duty of assistance always as part of a much broader project of helping *peoples* to attain liberal or decent institutions. As Leif Wenar has said of *The Law of Peoples:* "Rawls in this work is concerned more with the legitimacy of global coercion than he is with the arbitrariness of the fates of citizens of different countries."[39] As a result, the economic concerns of individuals play no role in Rawls's laws for regulating international relations. In the absence of mass starvation, or abuse of human rights, Rawls's principles of international justice do not extend to aiding individuals. As our world is now, however, millions will die from malnutrition and poverty-related illnesses before their countries gain liberal or decent institutions and become "well-ordered." To many, from the Secretary-General of the United Nations down, the issue of how the rich nations and their citizens are to respond to the needs of the more than one billion desperately poor people has an urgency that overrides the longer-term goal of changing the culture of societies that are not effectively regulated by a public conception of justice. But that issue is not one to which the author of *A Theory of Justice* has ever given serious attention.

The Reality

When subjected to the test of impartial assessment, there are few strong grounds for giving preference to the interests of one's fellow citizens, and none that can override the obligation that arises whenever we can, at little cost to ourselves, make an absolutely crucial difference to the well-being of another person in real need. Hence the issue of foreign aid is a matter with which citizens of any country of the developed world ought to be concerned. Citizens of the United States should feel particularly troubled about their country's contribution. Among the developed nations of the world, ranked according to the proportion of their Gross National Product that they give as development aid, the United States comes absolutely, indisputably, last.

Many years ago, the United Nations set a target for development aid of 0.7 percent of Gross National Product. A handful of developed nations—Denmark, The Netherlands, Norway and Sweden—meet or surpass this very modest target of giving 70 cents in every $100 that their economy produces to the developing nations. Most of them fail to reach it. Japan, for example, gives 0.27 percent. Overall, among the affluent nations, official development assistance fell from 0.33 percent of their combined GNP in 1985 to 0.22 percent in 2000. But of all the affluent nations, none fails so miserably to meet the United Nations target as the United States, which in 2000, the last year for which figures are available, gave 0.10 percent of GNP, or just 10 cents in every $100 its economy produces, one-seventh of the United Nations target. That is less *in actual U.S. dollars* than Japan gives—about $10 billion for the United States, as compared with $13.5 billion for Japan—although the U.S. economy is roughly twice the size of Japan's. And even that miserly sum exaggerates the U.S. aid to the most needy, for much of it is strategically targeted for political purposes. The largest single recipient of U.S. official development assistance is Egypt. (Russia and Israel get even more aid from the United States than Egypt, but it is not classified as development assistance.) Tiny Bosnia and Herzegovina gets a larger allocation from the United States than India. Japan, on the other hand, gives to Indonesia, China, Thailand, India, the Philippines, and Vietnam, in that order. India, for instance, gets more than five times as much assistance from Japan as it gets from the United States. Only a quarter of U.S. aid, as compared to more than half of Japan's aid, goes to low-income countries.[40]

When I make these points to audiences in the United States, some object that to focus on official aid is misleading. The United States, they say, is a country that does not believe in leaving everything to the government, as some other nations do. If private aid sources were also included, the United States would turn out to be exceptionally generous in its aid to other nations. So I checked private aid as well.[41] Yes, a higher proportion of the total aid given by the United States is non-government aid than is the case for other nations. But non-government aid everywhere is dwarfed by government aid, and that is true in the United States too, where non-government aid amounts to $4 billion, or about 40 percent of government aid.[42] So adding in the non-government aid takes the United States aid total only from 0.10 percent of GNP to 0.14 percent of GNP. This is still only one-fifth of the modest United Nations target, and not enough to get the United States off the very bottom of the table. While the United States gives $14 billion in private and official development aid each year, annual domestic U.S. spending on alcohol is $34 billion, on tobacco $32 billion, on non-alcoholic beverages, $26 billion, and on entertainment admission and fees, nearly $50 billion.[43] Turning to government spending, rather than general consumer expenditure, the Bush administration has proposed a military budget of $379 billion for the fiscal year 2003, an increase of $48 billion on the previous year's figure.[44] The increase alone is more than four times the amount the government gives in foreign aid. (Although President George W. Bush has also indicated that he would like to increase foreign aid by $5 billion over three years, this increase will not come into effect until 2004 and is dwarfed by the proposed increase in military spending.[45]) On the other hand, in each of the twelve years that followed the collapse of the Soviet Union in 1989, the U.S. government reaped a "peace dividend" that saved it, in military spending, at least six times—and in some years much more—the total amount it gave in foreign aid.[46] Even with the proposed increase for 2003, the U.S. government will still save, as compared with the military expenditures of the later years of the Reagan administration, an amount greater than the total foreign aid budget. None of this peace dividend has been used to boost foreign aid.

These facts are consistent with the claim made at the start of this chapter: despite the lip-service most people pay to human equality, their circle of concern barely extends beyond the boundary of their country. Yet not all the facts point to this bleak verdict. In 1995 the University of Maryland's Program on International Policy Attitudes, or PIPA, asked Americans what they thought about the amount that the United States was spending on foreign aid. A strong majority of those answering thought that the United States was spending too much on foreign aid and that aid should be cut. That response will make the cynics feel justified in their low opinion of human altruism, but when asked to estimate how much of the federal budget (not of GNP) was devoted to foreign aid, the median estimate—that is, the one in the middle of all the responses—was 15 percent. The correct answer is less than 1 percent. And when asked what an appropriate percentage would be, the median response was 5 percent—an increase on the amount actually spent that is beyond the wildest hopes of any foreign aid advocates on Capitol Hill. A few months later the *Washington Post* decided to run its own survey to see if the results held up. It got an even higher median estimate, that 20 percent of the federal budget was spent on foreign aid, and a median "right amount" of 10 percent. Some skeptics thought that the figure might be explained by the fact that people were including military expenditure in defense of other countries, but further research showed that this was not the case.

In 2000, PIPA asked a different sample the same questions. The most striking difference was that the strong majority (64 percent) that had in 1995 wanted U.S. foreign aid cut had shrunk to 40 percent. But when asked how much of the federal budget goes to foreign aid, the public was no better educated than before. The median estimate was 20 percent, the same as in the 1995 *Washington Post* survey. Only one respondent in 20 gave an estimate of 1 percent or less. Even among those with post-graduate education, the median estimate was 8 percent. Asked what would be an appropriate percentage, the median answer was again the same as that found by the earlier *Washington Post* survey, 10 percent.

The U.S. public's misperceptions about foreign aid have been confirmed in other surveys. A 1997 survey by the *Washington Post*, the Kaiser Family Foundation, and Harvard University listed five programs and asked which were the largest areas of spending by the federal government. Foreign aid ranked first, followed by Defense and Social Security. In fact, Defense and Social Security between them make up more than a third of the federal budget; foreign aid is insignificant by comparison. In the same year a Pew survey showed that 63 percent of Americans thought that the federal government spends more on foreign aid than it spends on Medicare, when Medicare spending is ten times foreign aid spending.[47]

The 2000 PIPA survey was held shortly after the United Nations Millennium Summit, at which the nations of the world set themselves a series of goals: to halve the proportion of people who suffer from hunger, or who live on less than $1 per day; to see that all children have a primary education; to reduce by two-thirds the under-five child mortality rate; to halve the proportion of people without access to safe drinking water; and to combat HIV/AIDS, malaria, and other diseases. The survey showed strong support for these goals, with 83 percent saying that they supported U.S. participation in an international effort to cut world hunger in half by 2015, and 75 percent saying that they would be willing to pay an extra $50 a year toward such a program. The World Bank has estimated that achieving the millennium development goals would cost $40 to 60 billion a year in additional aid for the next fifteen years.[48] If 75 percent of Americans over 18 years old were to contribute $50, more than $7.5 billion a year would be raised—not quite enough for America's share of the additional sum needed, but a good start.[49] It would, of course, be fairer if Americans with high incomes contributed more than $50, and those on lower incomes contributed less or nothing at all; but here I am simply noting what people have said about their willingness to help those in need, outside their country's borders.

Survey results should always be treated with caution, especially when asking about attitudes on topics where people may like to present themselves as more generous than they really are, but it is hard to dismiss the consistent findings that Americans are woefully ignorant about their country's dismal foreign aid record. What people would really want to do, once they knew the truth, is less clear. They have not been offered an opportunity to vote on the issue. No recent American president, or presidential contender with realistic prospects of success, has even tried to make foreign aid a major policy issue. America's failure to pull its weight in the fight against poverty is, therefore, due not only to the ignorance of the American public but also to the moral deficiencies of its political leaders.

An Ethical Challenge

If America's leaders continue to give only the most trifling attention to the needs of everyone except Americans (and the leaders of other rich nations continue to do only a little better) what should the citizens of those rich countries do? We are not powerless to act on our own. We can take practical steps to expand our concern across national boundaries by supporting organizations working to aid those in need, wherever they may be. But how much should we give?

More than 700 years ago Thomas Aquinas, later canonized by the Catholic Church, faced up to this question without flinching. Material goods are, he wrote, provided for the satisfaction of human needs and should not be divided in a way that hinders that goal. From this he drew the logical conclusion: "whatever a man has in superabundance is owed, of natural right, to the poor for their sustenance." Although Thomas Aquinas has had a major influence on the thinking of the Roman Catholic Church—to such an extent that "Thomism" has been described as the official philosophy of the Church—this particular aspect of his teachings is not one that the Church has chosen to emphasize. But how exactly we are to justify keeping what we have in "superabundance" when others are starving is not so easy to say.

In his book *Living High and Letting Die* New York philosopher Peter Unger presents an ingenious series of imaginary examples designed to probe our intuitions about whether it is wrong to live well without giving substantial amounts of money to help people who are hungry, malnourished, or dying from easily treatable illnesses like diarrhea. Here is my paraphrase of one of these examples.

> Bob is close to retirement. He has invested most of his savings in a very rare and valuable old car, a Bugatti, which he has not been able to insure. The Bugatti is his pride and joy. In addition to the pleasure he gets from driving and caring for his car, Bob knows that its rising market value means that he will always be able to sell it and live comfortably after retirement. One day when Bob is out for a drive, he parks the Bugatti near the end of a disused railway siding and goes for a walk up the track. As he does so, he sees that a runaway train, with no one aboard, is running down the railway track. Looking further down the track he sees the small figure of a child playing in a tunnel and very likely to be killed by the runaway train. He can't stop the train and the child is too far away to warn of the danger, but he can throw a switch that will divert the train down the siding where his Bugatti is parked. Then nobody will be killed—but since the barrier at the end of the siding is in disrepair, the train will destroy his Bugatti. Thinking of his joy in owning the car, and the financial security it represents, Bob decides not to throw the switch. The child is killed. But for many years to come Bob enjoys

owning his Bugatti and the financial security it
represents.[50]

Bob's conduct, most of us will immediately respond, was gravely
wrong. Unger agrees. But then he reminds us that we too have
opportunities to save the lives of children. We can give to organizations like UNICEF or Oxfam America. How much would
we have to give one of these organizations to have a high proba-
bility of saving the life of a child threatened by easily preventable
diseases?

In its fund-raising material, the U.S. Committee for UNICEF
says that a donation of $17 will provide immunization "to pro-
tect a child for life against the six leading child-killing and maim-
ing diseases: measles, polio, diphtheria, whooping cough, teta-
nus, and tuberculosis," while a donation of $25 will provide
"over 400 packets of oral rehydration salts to help save the lives
of children suffering from diarrheal dehydration." But these figures do not tell us how many lives are saved by the immunization
or rehydration salts, and they do not include the cost of raising
the money, administrative expenses, and delivering aid where it is
most needed. Unger called some experts to get a rough estimate
of these costs and the number of lives likely to be saved and came
up with a figure of around $200 per child's life saved. Assuming
that this estimate is not too far astray, if you still think that it was
very wrong of Bob not to throw the switch that would have diverted the train and saved the child's life, then it is hard to see
how you could deny that it is also very wrong not to send at least
$200 to one of the organizations listed above. Unless, that is, there
is some morally important difference between the two situations.
What might that be? Is it the practical uncertainties about whether
aid will really reach the people who need it? Nobody who knows
the world of overseas aid can doubt that such uncertainties exist.

But Unger's figure of $200 to save a child's life was reached after he had made conservative assumptions about the proportion of the money donated that will actually reach its target. One genuine difference between Bob and those who can donate to overseas aid organizations but don't is that only Bob can save the child in the tunnel, whereas there are hundreds of millions of people who can give $200 to overseas aid organizations. The problem is that most of them aren't doing it. Does this mean that it is all right not to do it?

Suppose that there were more owners of priceless vintage cars—Carol, Dave, Emma, Fred, and so on, down to Ziggy—all in exactly the same situation as Bob, with their own siding and their own switch, all sacrificing the child in order to preserve their own cherished car. Would that make it all right for Bob to do the same? To answer this question affirmatively is to endorse follow-the-crowd ethics—the kind of ethics that led many Germans to look away when the Nazi atrocities were being committed. We do not excuse them because others were behaving no better.

We seem to lack a sound basis for drawing a clear moral line between Bob's situation and that of anyone with $200 to spare who does not donate it to an overseas aid agency. These people seem to be acting at least as badly as Bob was acting when he chose to let the runaway train hurtle toward the unsuspecting child. Indeed, they seem to be behaving far worse, because for most Americans, to part with $200 is far less of a sacrifice than Bob would have to make to save the child. So it seems that we must be doing something seriously wrong if we are not prepared to give $200 to UNICEF or Oxfam America to reduce the poverty that causes so many early deaths. Since there are a lot of very needy children in the world, however, this is not the end of the moral claims on us. There will always be another child whose life you could save for another $200. Are we therefore obliged to keep giving until we have nothing left? At what point can we stop?

Consider Bob. How far past losing the Bugatti should he go? Imagine that Bob had got his foot stuck in the track of the siding, and if he diverted the train, then it would amputate his big toe before going on to ram his car. Should he still throw the switch? What if it would amputate his foot? His entire leg? Only when the sacrifices become very significant indeed would most people be prepared to say that Bob does nothing wrong when he decides not to throw the switch. Of course, most people could be wrong; we can't decide moral issues by taking opinion polls. But consider for yourself the level of sacrifice that you would demand of Bob, and then think about how much money you would have to give away in order to make a sacrifice that is roughly equal to that. It's almost certainly much, much more than $200. For most middle-class Americans, it could easily be more like $200,000. When Bob first grasped the dilemma that faced him as he stood by that railway switch, he must have thought how extraordinarily unlucky he was, to be placed in a situation in which he must choose between the life of an innocent child and the sacrifice of most of his savings. But he was not unlucky at all. We are all in that situation.

Some critics have questioned the factual assumptions behind such arguments. There is, they insist, an empirical question to be answered: "How much will each additional dollar of aid, given by me or by my government, contribute to the long-term well-being of people in areas receiving that aid?" It is not enough to find out the cost of delivering a packet of oral rehydration salts to a child who, without it, will die from diarrhea. We must look beyond saving life, to how the lives that are saved will be lived, to see if we have some reason to believe that saving the child will do more than perpetuate the cycle of poverty, misery, and high infant mortality.[51]

A World Bank study, *Assessing Aid,* points out that foreign aid has been both a "spectacular success" and an "unmitigated failure." On the success side:

> Internationally funded and coordinated programs have dramatically reduced such diseases as river blindness and vastly expanded immunization against key childhood diseases. Hundreds of millions of people have had their lives touched, if not transformed, by access to schools, clean water, sanitation, electric power, health clinics, roads, and irrigation—all financed by foreign aid.[52]

Among the failures is the aid that went to Zaire, now the Democratic Republic of the Congo, under the dictatorship of Mobutu. Corruption, incompetence, and misguided policies ensured that it had no impact. Extensive road building in Tanzania failed to improve the road network, because the roads were not maintained. But the World Bank study indicates that we now know more about what will work and what will not. It finds that when a poor country with good management is given aid equivalent to 1 percent of its GDP, poverty and infant mortality falls by 1 percent.[53] A more recent World Bank study has confirmed that the efficacy of aid is improving. Whereas in 1990 $1 billion in aid was sufficient to lift an estimated 105,000 people out of poverty, by 1997 to 1998 the same amount was lifting approximately 284,000 people out of poverty.[54] The tragedy is, as Joseph Stiglitz (then Chief Economist of the World Bank) points out in his foreword to the study, that "just as aid is poised to be its most effective, the volume of aid is declining and is at its lowest level ever."[55]

It is true that in the past government foreign aid has not been as effective in reducing poverty as one might hope. That is, to a significant extent, because it has not been aimed at reducing poverty. In a study titled "Who Gives Foreign Aid to Whom and

Why?" Alberto Alesina and David Dollar found that three of the biggest donors—the United States, France, and Japan—direct their aid, not to those countries where it will be most effective in fostering growth and reducing poverty, but to countries where aid will further their own strategic or cultural interests. The United States gives much of its aid to its friends in the Middle East, Israel and Egypt. Japan favors those countries that vote the way it votes in international forums like the United Nations. France gives overwhelmingly to its former colonies. The Nordic countries are the most notable exception to this pattern—they give to countries that are poor but have reasonably good governments that will not misuse the resources given.[56] Only when the biggest donors follow the example of the Nordic countries will we be able to tell how effective government foreign aid can be. Experienced non-government organizations, such as the various national members of the Oxfam International group, provide another model. They have had 50 years of experience in the field and have the ability to learn from their mistakes. There is always more to learn, but there is little doubt that well-intentioned, well-resourced, intelligent people, experienced in the cultural context in which they are working, can do a significant amount of good for those living in extreme poverty.[57]

A different objection to the argument that Unger and I have been putting forward is that it is poor policy to advocate a morality that most people will not follow. If we come to believe that, unless we make real sacrifices for strangers, we are doing wrong, then our response may be, not to give more, but to be less observant of other moral rules that we had previously followed. Making morality so demanding threatens to bring the whole of morality into disrepute. This objection effectively concedes that we ought to do a great deal more than we are now doing but denies that advocating this will really lead to the poor getting more assistance. The question then becomes: What policy will produce the best consequences? If it is true that advocating a highly demanding morality will lead to worse consequences than advocating a less demanding morality, then indeed we ought to advocate a less demanding morality. We could do this, while still knowing that, at the level of critical thinking, impartialism is sound. Here Sidgwick's point holds good: there is a distinction between "what it may be right to do, and privately recommend," and "what it would not be right to advocate openly."[58] We might, among ourselves, feel that we should forgo all "superabundance" in order to help those who are unable to provide for their bare subsistence, whereas in public we might decide to advocate whatever level of giving we believe will yield the greatest amount of assistance, while not making people feel that morality is so demanding that they will disregard it. If, by advocating that people give $50 a year—just $1 a week—to help the world's poorest people, it really were possible to get donations from the 75 percent of Americans that the 2000 PIPA survey suggested might be willing to give this sum, then that would be a target worth campaigning for. If it were possible to get $100 a year from, say, 60 percent of Americans, that would be better still, especially if the 15 percent willing to give $50 but not $100 would still give their $50. The point is to nominate as a target the figure that will lead to the greatest amount of money being raised. For that it needs to be a target that makes sense to people.

One way of looking at how much we might suggest that people should give is to suppose that the task of eliminating poverty in the world were fairly distributed among all of the 900 million people in high-income countries. How much would each of them have to give? As we have seen, the World Bank estimates that it would cost $40 to $60 billion per year in additional aid to achieve the development goals set at the United Nations Millennium Summit. These goals, calling for poverty and hunger to be halved by 2015, are more modest than the elimination of poverty. They could leave untouched the situation of the poorest of all, in countries where the costs of reaching poor people are higher than they are in countries with better infrastructures. But they are at least a stepping stone on the way to a more complete victory over poverty, so let us ask how much it would require, per person, to raise this sum. There are about 900 million people in the developed world, roughly 600 million of them adults. Hence a donation of about $100 per adult per year for the next fifteen years could achieve the Millennium Summit goals, even at the high end of the World Bank estimates. For someone earning $27,500 per annum, the average salary in the developed world, this is less than 0.4 percent of their annual income, or less than 1 cent in every $2 they earn.

There are many complexities that such figures ignore, but they go both ways. Not all residents of rich countries have income to spare, after meeting their basic needs; but on the other hand, there are hundreds of millions of rich people who live in poor countries, and they could and should give too. We could, therefore, advocate that everyone with income to spare, after meeting their family's basic needs, should contribute a minimum of 0.4 percent of their income to organizations working to help the world's poorest people. But to do so would be to set our sights too low, for it would take fifteen years even to halve poverty and hunger. During those fifteen years, tens of thousands of children will continue to die every day from poverty-related causes. We should feel a greater sense of urgency to eliminate poverty. Moreover there is nothing especially memorable about 0.4 percent of one's income. A more useful symbolic figure would be 1 percent, and this might indeed be closer to what it would take to eliminate, rather than halve, global poverty.

We could therefore propose, as a public policy likely to produce good consequences, that anyone who has enough money
to spend on the luxuries and frivolities so common in affluent
societies should give at least 1 cent in every dollar of their income
to those who have trouble getting enough to eat, clean water to
drink, shelter from the elements, and basic health care. Those
who do not meet this standard should be seen as failing to meet
their fair share of a global responsibility, and therefore as doing
something that is seriously morally wrong. This is the minimum,
not the optimal, donation. Those who think carefully about their
ethical obligations will realize that—since not everyone will be
giving even 1 percent—they should do far more. But if, for the
purposes of changing our society's standards in a manner that has
a realistic chance of success, we focus on the idea of a bare minimum that we can expect everyone to do, there is something to be
said for seeing a 1 percent donation of annual income to overcome world poverty as the minimum that one must do to lead a
morally decent life. To give that amount requires no moral hero-
ics. To fail to give it shows indifference to the indefinite continu-
ation of dire poverty and avoidable, poverty-related deaths.

In the light of such calculations of the amount of aid needed, it
is indicative of the present pessimistic climate of opinion about
aid that the targets set by the world leaders at the Millennium
Summit are commonly referred to as "ambitious."[59] Of course,
those who are skeptical about achieving them may be right—certainly the money that has been given or pledged to date falls far
short of what is needed. The $5 billion increase in U.S. aid over
three years pledged by President George W. Bush in March 2002,
while better than no increase at all, is nothing like the doubling of
foreign aid from rich countries sought by World Bank President
James D. Wolfensohn. The philanthropist George Soros called it,
with some justification, "a token gesture instead of something

that could successfully impact most of the poor countries."[60] By contrast, all it would take to put the world on track to eliminate global poverty much faster than the Millennium Summit targets would be the modest sum of 1 percent of annual income—if everyone who can afford it were to give it. That, as much as anything, tells us how far we still are from having an ethic that is based not on national boundaries, but on the idea of one world.

6   a better world?

In the fifth century before the Christian era, the Chinese philosopher Mozi, appalled at the damage caused by war in his era, asked: "What is the way of universal love and mutual benefit?" He answered his own question: "It is to regard other people's countries as one's own."[1] The ancient Greek iconoclast Diogenes, when asked what country he came from, is said to have replied: "I am a citizen of the world."[2] In the late twentieth century John Lennon sang that it isn't hard to "Imagine there's no countries . . . Imagine all the people/Sharing all the world."[3] Until recently such thoughts have been the dreams of idealists, devoid of practical impact on the hard realities of a world of nation-states. But now we are beginning to live in a global community. Almost all the nations of the world have reached a binding agreement about their greenhouse gas emissions. The global economy has given rise to the World Trade Organization, the World Bank, and the International Monetary Fund, institutions that take on, if imperfectly, some functions of global economic governance. An international criminal court is beginning its work. Changing ideas about military intervention for humanitarian purposes show we are in the process of developing a global community prepared to accept its responsibility to protect the citizens of states that cannot or will not protect them from massacre or genocide. In ringing declarations and resolutions, most recently at the United Nations Millennium Summit, the world's leaders have recognized that relieving the plight of the world's poorest nations is a global responsibility—although their deeds are yet to match their words.

When different nations led more separate lives, it was more understandable—though still quite wrong—for those in one country to think of themselves as owing no obligations, beyond that of non-interference, to people in another state. But those times are long gone. Today, as we have seen, our greenhouse gas emissions alter the climate under which everyone in the world lives. Our purchases of oil, diamonds, and timber make it possible for dictators to buy more weapons and strengthen their hold on the countries they tyrannize. Instant communications show us how others live, and they in turn learn about us and aspire to our way of life. Modern transport can move even relatively poor people thousands of miles, and when people are desperate to improve their situation, national boundaries prove permeable. As Branko Milanovic has argued, "It is unrealistic to hold that the large income differences between the Northern and Southern shores of the Mediterranean, or between Mexico and the United States, or between Indonesia and Malaysia, can continue without adding further pressure to migrate."[4]

The era that followed the Treaty of Westphalia (in 1648) was the high-water mark of the independent sovereign state. Behind the supposed inviolability of national borders, liberal democratic institutions took hold in some countries, while in others, rulers carried out genocide against their own citizens. At intervals, bloody wars broke out between the independent nation-states. Though we may look back on that era with some nostalgia, we should not regret its passing. Instead we should be developing the ethical foundations of the coming era of a single world community.

There is one great obstacle to further progress in this direction. It has to be said, in cool but plain language, that in recent years the international effort to build a global community has been hampered by the repeated failure of the United States to play its part. Despite being the single largest polluter of the world's atmosphere, and on a per capita basis the most profligate of the major nations, the United States has refused to join the 178 states that have accepted the Kyoto Protocol. Along with Libya and China, the United States voted against setting up an International Criminal Court to try people accused of genocide and crimes against humanity. Now that the court seems likely to go ahead, the U.S. government has said that it has no intention of participating. The United States has consistently failed to pay the dues it owes to the United Nations, and in November 2001, even after paying off a portion of its debt in the wake of the September 11 attacks, it still owed that institution $1.07 billion. Though it is one of the world's wealthiest nations, with the world's strongest economy, the United States gives significantly less foreign aid, as a proportion of its Gross National Product, than any other developed nation. When the world's most powerful state wraps itself in what—until September 11, 2001—it took to be the security of its military might, and arrogantly refuses to give up any of its own rights and privileges for the sake of the common good—even when other nations are giving up their rights and privileges—the prospects of finding solutions to global problems are dimmed. One can only hope that when the rest of the world nevertheless proceeds down the right path, as it did in resolving to go ahead with the Kyoto Protocol, and as it is now doing with the International Criminal Court, the United States will eventually be shamed into joining in. If it does not, it risks falling into a situation in which it is universally seen by everyone except its own self-satisfied citizens as the world's "rogue superpower." Even from a strictly self-interested perspective, if the United States wants the cooperation of other nations in matters that are largely its own concern—such as the struggle to eliminate terrorism—it cannot afford to be so regarded.

I have argued that as more and more issues increasingly demand global solutions, the extent to which any state can independently determine its future diminishes. We therefore need to strengthen institutions for global decision-making and make them more responsible to the people they affect. This line of thought leads in the direction of a world community with its own directly elected legislature, perhaps slowly evolving along the lines of the European Union. There is little political support for such ideas at present. Apart from the threat that the idea poses to the self-interest of the citizens of the rich nations, many would say it puts too much at risk, for gains that are too uncertain. It is widely believed that a world government will be, at best, an unchecked bureaucratic behemoth that makes the bureaucracy of the European Union look like a lean and efficient operation. At worst, it will become a global tyranny, unchecked and unchallengeable.

These thoughts have to be taken seriously. How to prevent global bodies becoming either dangerous tyrannies or self-aggrandizing bureaucracies, and instead make them effective and responsive to the people whose lives they affect, is something that we still need to learn. It is a challenge that should not be beyond the best minds in the fields of political science and public administration, once they adjust to the new reality of the global community and turn their attention to issues of government beyond national boundaries. We need to learn from the experience of other multinational organizations. The European Union is a federal body that has adopted the principle that decisions should always be taken at the lowest level capable of dealing with the problem. The application of this principle, known as subsidiarity, is still being tested. But if it works for Europe, it is not impossible that it might work for the world.[5]

To rush into world federalism would be too risky, but we could accept the diminishing significance of national boundaries and take a pragmatic, step-by-step approach to greater global governance. The preceding chapters have argued that there is a good case for global environmental and labor standards. The World Trade Organization has indicated its support for the International Labor Organization to develop core labor standards. If these standards are developed and accepted, they would not be much use without a global body to check that they are being adhered to, and to allow other countries to impose trade sanctions against goods that are not produced in conformity with the standards. Since the WTO seems eager to pass this task over to the ILO, we might see that organization significantly strengthened. Something similar could happen with environmental standards. It is even possible to imagine a United Nations Economic and Social Security Council that would take charge of the task of eliminating global poverty, and would be voted the resources to do it.[6] These and other specific proposals for stronger global institutions to accomplish a particular task should be considered on their merits.

The fifteenth and sixteenth centuries are celebrated for the voyages of discovery that proved that the world is round. The eighteenth century saw the first proclamations of universal human rights. The twentieth century's conquest of space made it possible for a human being to look at our planet from a point not on it, and so to see it, literally, as one world. Now the twenty-first century faces the task of developing a suitable form of government for that single world. It is a daunting moral and intellectual challenge, but one we cannot refuse to take up. The future of the world depends on how well we meet it.

notes

1 a changing world

1. *New York Times*, 30 March 2001, p. A11.
2. David Rosenbaum, "Senate Deletes Higher Mileage Standard in Energy Bill," *New York Times*, 14 March 2002, p. A28.
3. Philip Elmer-Dewitt, "Summit to Save the Earth: Rich vs. Poor," *Time*, 139:2, June 1992, pp. 42–48, www.cddc.vt.edu/tim/tims/Tim599.htm.
4. Bill Keller, "The World According to Colin Powell," *New York Times Sunday Magazine*, 25 November 2001, p. 67.
5. *Report of the Independent Inquiry into the Actions of the United Nations During the 1994 Genocide in Rwanda*, United Nations, Office of the Spokesman for the Secretary-General, New York, 15 December 1999, www.un.org/News/ossg/rwanda_report.htm.
6. Kofi Annan, "Two Concepts of Sovereignty," *The Economist* 18 September 1999, www.un.org/Overview/SG/kaecon.htm.
7. John Langdon, *July 1914: The Long Debate, 1918–1990*, Berg, New York, 1991, p. 175.
8. G. P. Gooch and H. Temperley, eds., *British Documents on the Origins of the War, 1898–1914*, London, 1926–1938, vol. XI, no. 91; cited in Zara Steiner, *Britain and the Origins of the First World War*, St. Martin's Press, New York, 1977, pp. 221–222.

9. Charles Horne, ed., *Source Records of the Great War,* vol. I, The American Legion, Indianapolis, 1931, p. 285

10. Security Council Resolution 1373 (2001), www.un.org/Docs/scres/2001/res1373e.pdf.

11. Report of the High-Level Panel on Financing for Development appointed by the United Nations Secretary-General, United Nations General Assembly, Fifty-fifth Session, Agenda item 101, 26 June 2001, A/55/1000, p. 3, www.un.org/esa/ffd/a55-1000.pdf.

12. Juliet Eilperin, "House Approves U.N. Payment Legislation Would Provide $582 Million for Back Dues," *Washington Post,* 25 September 2001, p. A01.

13. See John Rawls, *A Theory of Justice,* Oxford University Press, Oxford, 1971. The objection to Rawls that I have put here was made by Brian Barry in *The Liberal Theory of Justice,* Oxford University Press, Oxford, 1973, pp. 129–130. See also the same author's *Theories of Justice,* University of California Press, Berkeley, 1989. Other arguments to the same end have been pressed by Charles Beitz, *Political Theory and International Relations,* Princeton University Press, Princeton, 1979, and "Social and Cosmopolitan Liberalism," *International Affairs,* 75:3, 1999, pp. 515–529; by Thomas Pogge, *Realizing Rawls,* Cornell University Press, Ithaca, N.Y., 1990, and "An Egalitarian Law of Peoples," *Philosophy and Public Affairs,* 23:3, 1994; and by Andrew Kuper, "Rawlsian Global Justice: Beyond *The Law of Peoples* to a Cosmopolitan Law of Persons," *Political Theory* 28:5, 2000, pp. 640–674.

14. "The Poverty of Philosophy," in David McLellan, ed., Karl Marx: *Selected Writings,* Oxford University Press, Oxford, 1977, p. 202.

15. Thomas Friedman, *The Lexus and the Olive Tree,* Anchor Books, New York, 2000, pp. 104–106.

16. Friedman, *Lexus and the Olive Tree,* p. 112.

17. Friedman, *Lexus and the Olive Tree,* p. 104.

18. On the evolution of ethics, see Peter Singer, *The Expanding Circle,* Farrar, Straus and Giroux, New York, 1981. On globalization as the basis for a new ethic, see Clive Kessler, "Globalization: Another False Universalism?," *Third World Quarterly,* 21, 2000, pp. 931–942.

2 one atmosphere

1. "This Year Was the 2nd Hottest, Confirming a Trend, UN Says," *New York Times*, 19 December 2001, p. A5.

2. J. T. Houghton et al., eds., *Climate Change 2001: The Scientific Basis: Contribution of Working Group I to the Third Assessment Report of the Intergovernmental Panel on Climate*, United Nations Environment Program and Intergovernmental Panel on Climate Change, Cambridge University Press, Cambridge, 2001, Summary for Policymakers; available at www.ipcc.ch/pub/tar/wg1/index. htm. See also *Reconciling Observations of Global Temperature Change*, Panel on Reconciling Temperature Observations, National Research Council, National Academy of Sciences, Washington, D.C., 2000, available at www.nap.edu/books/0309068916/html. For another example of recent research indicating that anthropogenic climate change is real, see Thomas J. Crowley, "Causes of Climate Change Over the Past 1000 Years," *Science*, 14 July 2000, 289: 270–277.

3. Houghton et al., eds., *Climate Change 2001: The Scientific Basis*.

4. Munich Reinsurance, one of the world's largest insurance companies, has estimated that the number of major natural disasters has risen from 16 in the 1960s to 70 in the 1990s. Cited by Christian Aid, Global Advocacy Team Policy Position Paper, *Global Warming, Unnatural Disasters and the World's Poor*, November 2000, www.christianaid.org.uk/indepth/0011glob/globwarm.htm.

5. James McCarthy et al., eds., *Climate Change 2001: Impacts, Adaptation, and Vulnerability, Contribution of Working Group II to the Third Assessment Report of the Intergovernmental Panel on Climate Change*, United Nations Environment Program and Intergovernmental Panel on Climate Change, Cambridge University Press, Cambridge, 2001, chapter 9.7; available at www.ipcc.ch/pub/tar/wg2/index.htm.

6. Houghton et al., eds., *Climate Change 2001: The Scientific Basis*.

7. See Dale Jamieson, "Ethics, Public Policy, and Global Warming," *Science, Technology, and Human Values* 17:2, Spring 1992, pp. 139–153, and "Global Responsibilities: Ethics, Public Health, and Global Environmental Change," *Indiana Journal of Global Legal Studies* 5:1, Fall 1997, pp. 99–119.

8. "Norway Wants Sanctions for Cross Border Polluters," *Reuters News*

Service, 1 February 2002, www.planetark.org/dailynewsstory.cfm/
newsid/14316/story.htm.

9. *United Nations Framework Convention on Climate Change,* Article 4,
section 2, subsections (a) and (b), available at www.unfccc.int/resource/
conv/conv.html; *Guide to the Climate Change Negotiation Process,*
www.unfccc.int/resource/process/components/response/respconv.html.

10. "U.S. Carbon Emissions Jump in 2000," *Los Angeles Times,* 11 November
2001, p. A36, citing figures released by the U.S. Department of Energy's
Energy Information Administration on 9 November 2001.

11. Eileen Claussen and Lisa McNeilly, *The Complex Elements of Global
Fairness,* Pew Center on Global Climate Change, Washington, D.C., 29
October 1998, www.pewclimate.org/projects/pol_equity.cfm.

12. Bjorn Lomborg, "The Truth about the Environment," *The Economist,* 2
August 2001, available at www.economist.com/science/
displayStory.cfm?Story_ID=718860&CFID=3046335&CFTOKEN=
88404876.

13. Bjorn Lomborg, *The Skeptical Environmentalist,* Cambridge University
Press, Cambridge, 2001, p. 323.

14. See Richard Newell and William Pizer, *Discounting the Benefits of Future
Climate Change Mitigation: How Much Do Uncertain Rates Increase
Valuations?* Pew Center on Global Climate Change, Washington, D.C.,
December 2001. Available at www.pewclimate.org/projects/
econ_discounting.cfm.

15. Robert Nozick, *Anarchy, State and Utopia,* Basic Books, New York, 1974,
p. 153.

16. John Locke, *Second Treatise on Civil Government,* C. B. Macpherson, ed.,
Hacket, Indianapolis, 1980, sec. 27, p. 19.

17. See Garrett Hardin, "The Tragedy of the Commons," *Science,* 162, 1968,
pp. 1243–1248.

18. Locke, *Second Treatise on Civil Government,* sec. 41.

19. Adam Smith, *A Theory of the Moral Sentiments,* Prometheus, Amherst,
N.Y., 2000, IV, i. 10.

20. Peter Hayes and Kirk Smith, eds., *The Global Greenhouse Regime: Who
Pays?* Earthscan, London, 1993, chapter 2, table 2.4, /80836E00.htm;
available at www.unu.edu/unupress/unupbooks/80836e/
80836E08.htm.

21. See S. Fan, M. Gloor, J. Mahlman, S. Pacala, J. Sarmiento, T. Takahashi,

and P. Tans, "A Large Terrestrial Carbon Sink in North America Implied by Atmospheric and Oceanic Carbon Dioxide Data and Models," *Science*, 282, 16 October 1998, pp. 442–446.

22. William Schlesinger and John Lichter, "Limited Carbon Storage in Soil and Litter of Experimental Forest Plots under Increased Atmospheric CO2," *Nature*, 411, 24 May 2001, pp. 466–469.

23. Duncan Austin, José Goldemberg, and Gwen Parker, "Contributions to Climate Change: Are Conventional Metrics Misleading the Debate?," World Resource Institute Climate Protection Initiative, Climate Notes, www.igc.org/wri/cpi/notes/metrics.html.

24. The Intergovernmental Panel on Climate Change, *First Assessment Report* was published in three volumes. See especially J. T. Houghton, G. J. Jenkins, and J. J. Ephraums, eds., *Scientific Assessment of Climate Change-Report of Working Group I,* Cambridge University Press, Cambridge, 1990. For details of the other volumes see www.ipcc.ch/pub/reports.htm.

25. See G. Marland, T. A. Boden, and R. J. Andres, *Global, Regional, and National Fossil Fuel CO2 Emissions,* Carbon Dioxide Information Analysis Center, Oak Ridge, Tennessee, available at cdiac.esd.ornl.gov/trends/emis/top96.cap. These are 1996 figures.

26. Paul Baer et al., "Equity and Greenhouse Gas Responsibility," *Science* 289, 29 September 2000, p. 2287; Dale Jamieson, "Climate Change and Global Environmental Justice," in P. Edwards and C. Miller, eds., *Changing the Atmosphere: Expert Knowledge and Global Environmental Governance,* MIT Press, Cambridge, Mass., 2001, pp. 287–307.

27. See John Rawls, *A Theory of Justice,* especially pp. 65–83. For a different way of giving priority to the worst-off, see Derek Parfit, "Equality or Priority?," The Lindley Lecture, University of Kansas, 21 November 1991, reprinted in Matthew Clayton and Andrew Williams, eds., *The Ideal of Equality,* Macmillan, London, 2000.

28. This is Rawls's "difference principle," applied without the restriction to national boundaries that are difficult to defend in terms of his own argument. See chapter 5 for further discussion of this point.

29. "President Announces Clear Skies and Global Climate Change Initiative," Office of the Press Secretary, White House, 14 February 2002, www.whitehouse.gov/news/releases/2002/02/20020214-5.html. For amplification of the basis of the administration's policy, see Executive Office of the President, Council of Economic Advisers, *2002 Economic*

Report of the President, U.S. Government Printing Office, Washington, D.C., 2002, chapter 6, pp. 244–249, http://w3.access.gpo.gov/eop/.

30. National Council on Economic Education, "A Case Study: United States International Trade in Goods and Services—May 2001," www.econedlink.org/lessons/index.cfm?lesson=EM196.

31. Andrew Revkin, "Sliced Another Way: Per Capita Emissions," *New York Times,* 17 June 2001, section 4, p. 5.

32. For discussion of equal votes as a compromise, see my *Democracy and Disobedience,* Clarendon Press, Oxford, 1973, pp. 30–41.

33. Energy Information Administration, *Emissions of Greenhouse Gases in the United States 2000,* DOE/EIA-0573 (2000), U.S. Department of Energy, Washington, D.C., November 2001, page vii, www.eia.doe.gov/pub/oiaf/1605/cdrom/pdf/ggrpt/057300.pdf.

34. See Jae Edmonds et al., *International Emissions Trading and Global Climate Change: Impacts on the Cost of Greenhouse Gas Mitigation.* A report prepared for the Pew Center on Global Climate Change, December 1999, available at www.pewclimate.org/projects/econ_emissions.cfm.

3 one economy

1. Tony Clarke, *By What Authority? Unmasking and Challenging the Global Corporations' Assault on Democracy through the World Trade Organization,* International Forum on Globalization and the Polaris Institute, San Francisco and Ottawa, no date (1999), p. 14.

2. Thomas Friedman, "Senseless in Seattle," *New York Times,* 1 December 1999, p. A23.

3. Victor Menotti, *Free Trade, Free Logging: How the World Trade Organization Undermines Global Forest Conservation,* International Forum on Globalization, San Francisco, 1999, p. ii.

4. *Agscene,* Autumn 1999, p. 20.

5. Martin Khor,"How the South Is Getting a Raw Deal at the WTO," in Sarah Anderson, ed., *Views from the South: The Effects of Globalization and the WTO on Third World Countries,* International Forum on Globalization, San Francisco, n.d. (1999), p. 11.

6. Vandana Shiva, "War Against Nature and the People of the South," in Anderson, *Views from the South,* pp. 92, 93, 123.

7. Thomas Friedman, *The Lexus and the Olive Tree,* Anchor Books, New York, 2000, p. 190.

8. See World Economic Forum, *Summaries of the Annual Meeting 2000,* Geneva (2000) summary of session 56.

9. World Trade Organization website, www.wto.org, 1.1.2002.

10. "The WTO in Brief, Part 3: The WTO Agreements," available at www.wto.org/english/thewto_e/whatis_e/inbrief_e/inbr03_e.htm.

11. *Ten Common Misunderstandings about the WTO,* WTO, Geneva, 1999, available at www.wto.org/english/thewto_e/whatis_e/10mis_e/10m00_e.htm.

12. World Trade Organization, Minsterial Declaration, 14 November 2001, paragraph 6, www-chil.wto-ministerial.org/english/thewto e/minist e/min01_c/mindecl_c.htm.

13. See www.wto.org/english/thewto_e/whatis_e/tif_e/bey5_e.htm.

14. See www.wto.org/english/thewto_e/whatis_e/tif_e/bey5_e.htm; italics in original.

15. Leesteffy Jenkins and Robert Stumberg, "Animal Protection in a World Dominated by the World Trade Organization," in Deborah Salem and Andrew Rowan, eds., *The State of the Animals 2001,* Humane Society Press, Washington, D.C., 2001, p. 149.

16. Salem and Rowan, *The State of the Animals,* p. 149. See also the United Kingdom Parliament's Select Committee on European Scrutiny Twenty-first Report, "Animal Testing and Cosmetic Products, available at www.parliament.the-stationery-office.co.uk/pa/cm199900/cmselect/cmeuleg/23-xxi/2303.htm.

17. Peter Stevenson, "GATT Implications for Animal Welfare in the European Union," a paper presented to the CIWF Trust Conference, April 1998, available at www.ciwf.co.uk/Pubs/Briefings/ART4173.htm.

18. Charles E. Hanrahan, "RS20142: The European Union's Ban on Hormone-Treated Meat" updated 19 December 2000, *Congressional Research Service Issue Brief,* www.cnie.org/nle/ag-63.html.

19. See www.wto.org/english/thewto_e/whatis_e/tif_e/bey5_e.htm.

20. World Trade Organization, WT/DS58/AB/R 12 October 1998 paragraph 165, www.wto.org/english/tratop_e/dispu_e/distab_e.htm. Paragraph numberings appear to differ in different electronic versions of this document.

21. "DSB Adopts Two Appellate Body Reports on Shrimp and Corn Syrup," *WTO News,* 21 November 2001, www.wto.org/english/news_e/ news01_e/dsb_21nov01_e.htm; *Bridges Weekly Trade News Digest,* vol. 5, no. 40, 28 November 2001.

22. Lori Wallach and Michelle Sforza, *Whose Trade Organization?,* Public Citizen, Inc., Washington, D.C., 1999, pp. 4–5.

23. Salem and Rowan, *The State of the Animals 2001,* p. 149.

24. World Trade Organization, Minsterial Declaration, 14 November 2001, WT/MIN(01)/DEC/1, paragraph 13, www-chil.wto-ministerial.org/ english/thewto_e/minist_e/min01_e/mindecl_e.htm.

25. See www.wto.org/english/thewto_e/whatis_e/10ben_e/10b10_e.htm.

26. See, for example, the *New York Times* editorial "The Urgency of Cheaper Drugs," 31 October 2001, p. A14, and Nicolo Itano, "Double Standards," *Christian Science Monitor,* 9 November 2001.

27. World Trade Organization, "Declaration on the TRIPS Agreement and Public Health," 14 November 2001, WT/MIN(01)/DEC/2, paragraphs 4, 5; www-chil.wto-ministerial.org/english/thewto_e/minist_e/ min01_e/mindecl_trips_e.htm.

28. Khor, "How the South Is Getting a Raw Deal at the WTO," in Anderson, *Views from the South,* p. 14; Walden Bello, "Building an Iron Cage: The Bretton Woods Institutions, the WTO and the South," in Anderson, *Views from the South,* pp. 85–86.

29. Frank Bruni and David Sanger, "Bush Urges Shift to Direct Grants for Poor Nations," *New York Times,* 18 July 2001, p. A1.

30. Anuradha Mittal, "The South in the North," in Anderson, *Views from the South,* pp. 168–169; cf. the previously cited essays by Walden Bello and Vandana Shiva, in the same volume.

31. Vandana Shiva, "War Against Nature and the People of the South," in Anderson, *Views from the South,* pp. 98, 99.

32. World Bank, *World Development Report 2000/2001,* Oxford University Press, New York, 2001, pp. 17, 23, 274–275, worldbank.org/poverty/ wdrpoverty/report/index.htim. The adjustment for cost of living between 1993 and 2000 comes from http://stats.bls.gov/cpihome.htm. These and several other figures in this section are cited in Thomas Pogge, "Global Poverty: Explanation and Responsibilities," a paper read at the 5th Annual Charles T. and Louise H. Travers Conference on Ethics and Government Accountability, held at the University of California,

Berkeley, in April 2001. Also from Pogge's paper is the estimate that the
average income of the world's poorest fifth is 30 percent below the
poverty line. He reaches this figure from data provided by Shaohua Chen
and Martin Ravallion, *How Did the World's Poorest Fare in the 1990's?*
Working Paper, August 2000, tables 2 and 4 (dividing the poverty gap
index by the headcount index). Chen and Ravallion's paper is available at
http://econ.worldbank.org/docs/1164.pdf.

33. United Nations Development Programme (UNDP), *Human
Development Report 2000*, Oxford University Press, New York, 2000,
p. 30; *Human Development Report 2001*, Oxford University Press, New
York, 2001, pp. 9–12, p. 22; and World Bank, *World Development Report
2000/2001*, Overview, p. 3; see www.worldbank.org/poverty/wdrpoverty/
report/overview.pdf for the other figures. The *Human Development
Reports* are available at www.undp.org/hdro/highlights/past.htm.

34. Robert McNamara in World Bank, *World Development Report 1978*,
World Bank, New York, 1978, p. iii.

35. World Bank, *World Development Report 2002*, Oxford University Press,
New York, 2001, econ.worldbank.org/wdr/structured_doc.php?pr=
2391&doc_id=2394, p. 233. See also World Bank, *World Development
Report 2000/2001*, New York, Oxford University Press, New York, 2001,
p. 275.

36. UNDP, *Human Development Report 1999*, Oxford University Press, New
York, 1999, pp. 3, 36.

37. Dan Ben-David, Hakan Nordström and Alan Winters, *Trade, Income
Disparity and Poverty*, World Trade Organization, 1999, p. 3,
www.wto.org/english/news_e/pres00_e/pov1_e.pdf, cited by Chantal
Thomas, "Global Economic Justice, Human Rights and the International
Trade Order," a paper read to the Global Justice Conference, Center for
Law and Philosophy, Columbia Law School, New York, 31 March 2001.

38. UNDP, *Human Development Report 1999*, p.3.

39. A. Melchior, K. Telle, and H. Wiig, "Globalisation and Inequality: World
Income Distribution and Living Standards, 1960–1998," Royal
Norwegian Ministry of Foreign Affairs, Studies on Foreign Policy Issues,
Report 6B, October 2000, http://odin.dep.no/archive/udvedlegg/01/
01/rev__016.pdf, pp.12, 15–17; UNDP, *Human Development Report 2001*,
p. 20. I owe this reference to Chantal Thomas, "Global Economic Justice,
Human Rights and the International Trade Order."

40. Branko Milanovic, "True World Income Distribution, 1988 and 1993: First Calculations Based on Household Surveys Alone," *The Economic Journal,* 112:1, 2002, pp. 51–92. For discussion, see Melchior, Telle, and Wiig, "Globalisation and Inequality," p. 18.

41. Milanovic, personal communication, August 2001.

42. Alberto Alesina and Roberto Perotti, "The Political Economy of Growth: A Critical Survey of the Recent Literature," *The World Bank Economic Review,* vol. 8, 1994, no. 3, pp. 350–371; Roberto Perotti, "Growth, Income Distribution and Democracy: What the Data Say," *Journal of Economic Growth,* vol. 1, 1996, pp. 149–187. I owe these references to Branko Milanovic.

43. United Nations, *Human Development Report 1997,* p. 2; cited by Friedman, *Lexus and the Olive Tree,* p. 350.

44. UNDP, *Human Development Report 1999,* p. 154.

45. Melchior, Telle, and Wiig, "Globalisation and Inequality," pp. 16–17, 21.

46. UNDP, *Human Development Report 1996,* p. 151; cited by Melchior, Telle, and Wiig, "Globalisation and Inequality," p. 25; cf. UNDP, *Human Development Report 2001,* pp. 11–12.

47. Melchior, Telle, and Wiig, "Globalisation and Inequality," p. 32, citing FAO 1999 figures.

48. Melchior, Telle, and Wiig, "Globalisation and Inequality," pp. 29–30, citing figures from UNDP, *Human Development Report 1996.*

49. World Bank, *World Development Report 2000/2001,* p. 23.

50. On the problems of assessing whether the number of poor people is increasing or decreasing, see Angus Deaton, "Counting the World's Poor: Problems and Possible Solutions," www.wws.princeton.edu:80/rpds/worldpov3b.pdf. Melchior, Telle, and Wiig, "Globalisation and Inequality," p. 22, agree that the methods currently available to us are inadequate for reaching a conclusion on this question. For a discussion of the complexities involved in deciding whether it is a good thing if there are more people in existence, see Derek Parfit, *Reasons and Persons,* Clarendon Press, Oxford, 1984, pt. IV.

51. "Foreign Friends," *The Economist,* 8 January 2000, pp. 71–72.

52. Peter Lindert and Jeffrey Williamson, "Does Globalization Make the World More Unequal?" NBER Working Paper Series, Working Paper 8228, National Bureau of Economic Research, Cambridge, Mass., April 2001. See papers.nber.org/papers/w8228.

53. Mattias Lundberg and Lyn Squire, "The Simultaneous Evolution of Growth and Inequality," pp. 27, 31; www.worldbank.org/research/ growth/pdfiles/squire.pdf.

54. Melchior, Telle, and Wiig, "Globalisation and Inequality," pp. 32–37.

55. BBC News, "Congo in Dire Trouble, Say Agencies," 7 August 2001, news.bbc.co.uk/hi/english/world/africa/newsid_1477000/1477003.stm.

56. Karl Marx, *Communist Manifesto,* Penguin, Harmondsworth, 1967, p. 82.

57. Herman E. Daly, "Globalization and Its Discontents," *Philosophy and Public Policy Quarterly,* 21, 2/3, 2001, p. 19.

58. Vandana Shiva, "Social Environment Clauses—A 'Political Diversion'," in *Third World Economics,* 118, 1996, pp. 8–9, as quoted in Michelle Swenarchuk, "The International Confederation of Free Trade Unions Labour Clause Proposal: A Legal and Political Critique," in Stephen McBride and John Wiseman, eds., *Globalisation and Its Discontents,* St. Martin's Press, New York, 2000, p. 167.

59. For the Singapore declaration, see World Trade Organization, Ministerial Declaration, 13 December 1996, WT/MIN(96)/DEC, paragraph 4, www.wto.org/english/thewto_e/minist_e/min96_e/wtodec_e.htm. For Doha, see World Trade Organization, Minsterial Declaration, 14 November 2001, WT/MIN(01)/DEC/1, paragraph 8, www-chil.wto-ministerial.org/english/thewto_e/minist_e/min01_e/mindecl_e.htm.

60. The agreement is available at member.nifty.ne.jp/menu/wto/1947/ 1947e36.htm. This clause could provide the legal basis for Thomas Pogge's proposal, in "A Global Resources Dividend" in David Crocker and Toby Linden, eds., *Ethics of Consumption: The Good Life, Justice and Global Stewardship,* Rowman and Littlefield, Lanham, Md., 1997, that states be required to share with the world's poor a small part of the value of any resources they use or sell.

61. *Economist,* 25 September 1999, p. 89, citing J. Michael Finger, and Philip Schuler, "Implementation of Uruguay Round Commitments: The Development Challenge," *World Bank Research Working Paper 2215,* econ.worldbank.org/docs/941.pdf. I owe this reference to Thomas Pogge, "Global Poverty: Explanation and Responsibility."

62. Joseph Kahn, "U.S. Sees Trade Talks as a Test of Leadership," *New York Times,* 9 November 2001, p. C6.

63. Thomas Hertel and Will Martin, "Would Developing Countries Gain from the Inclusion of Manufactures in the WTO Negotiations?,"

Working Paper 7, presented to the conference on WTO and the Millennium Round, Geneva, September 1999, http://ae761e.agecon. purdue.edu/gtap/resources/download/42.pdf.

64. World Trade Organization, "Background Paper: The WTO's 2-Year Strategy Comes to Fruition," January 2002, paragraph 17, available at www.wto.org/english/news_e/news_e.htm.

65. This issue was brought to my attention by Thomas Pogge, to whom the following discussion is indebted. See his "Achieving Democracy," *Ethics and International Affairs* 15:1, 2001, pp. 3–23, as well as his *World Poverty and Human Rights*, Blackwell, Cambridge, Mass., 2002, chapter 4.

66. Lassa Oppenheim, *International Law*, vol. I, London, Longmans, 1905, p. 403; cited by Gregory H. Fox, "The Right to Political Participation in International Law," in Cecelia Lynch and Michael Loriaux, eds., *Law and Moral Action in World Politics,* University of Minnesota Press, Minneapolis, 1999, p. 83.

67. Brad Roth, *Governmental Illegitimacy in International Law,* Clarendon Press, Oxford, 1999, pp. 162–163.

68. Thomas Jefferson to Gouverneur Morris, 7 November 1792, *Works,* fourth edition, vol. III, p. 489, cited in Roth, *Governmental Illegitimacy in International Law,* p. 321.

69. Anthony DePalma, "Talks Tie Trade in the Americas to Democracy," *New York Times,* 23 April 2001, p. A1.

70. Well, maybe not so basic—if the United States were to apply for admission to the European Union, its application would be rejected because the European Union considers the death penalty to be a violation of human rights. The European Union's position on the death penalty was re-affirmed in Article 2(2) of the EU Charter on Fundamental Freedoms signed at Nice in December 2000.

71. Severine M. Rugumamu, "State Sovereignty and Intervention in Africa: Nurturing New Governance Norms," Discussion paper presented to the International Commission on Intervention and State Sovereignty, Maputo, 10 March 2001, http://web.gc.cuny.edu/icissresearch/ maputu%20discussion%20paper%20nurturing%20new%20norms. htm#N_1_.

72. *Final Warsaw Declaration: Towards a Community of Democracies,* 27 June 2000, circulated by the United Nations Secretariat as General Assembly

Doc. A/55/328; available at www.democracyconference.org/
declaration.html.

73. Michael Ross, *Extractive Sectors and the Poor*, Oxfam America, Boston,
2001; available at www.eireview.org/eir/eirhome.nsf/(DocLibrary)/
6F177A935572B21785256AE3005AD736/$FILE/Oxfam_EI_Report.pdf;
Jeffrey Sachs and Andrew Warner, "Natural Resource Abundance and
Economic Growth," National Bureau of Economic Research Working
Paper 5398, 1995; available at http://papers.nber.org/papers/W5398.

74. See Pogge, *World Poverty and Human Rights*, chapter 4.

4 one law

1. Numbers 31:1–18, King James Version.

2. See, for example, Deuteronomy 3:1–7, 7:1–26, 20:13–17; I Samuel 15:3;
Joshua 8:26–28; Ezekiel 9:5.

3. Lawrence Keeley, *War Before Civilization*, Oxford University Press, New
York, 1996. See especially chapter 6.

4. Richard Wrangham and Dale Peterson, *Demonic Males: Apes and the
Origins of Human Violence*. Houghton Mifflin, Boston, 1996, pp. 5–21;
see also Jane Goodall, *The Chimpanzees of Gombe*, Belknap Press of
Harvard University Press, Cambridge, Mass., 1986, pp. 530–534.

5. The classic article on this topic is R. L. Trivers, "The Evolution of
Reciprocal Altruism," *Quarterly Review of Biology*, vol. 46, 1971, pp. 35–
57; see also Robert Axelrod, *The Evolution of Cooperation*, Basic Books,
New York, 1984.

6. Tony Ashworth, *Trench Warfare, 1914–1918: The Live and Let Live
Solution*, Holmes and Meier, New York, 1980.

7. Timothy Garton Ash, *History of the Present*, Allen Lane, London, 1999,
p. 368.

8. *Charter of the International Military Tribunal*, Article 6, www.yale.edu/
lawweb/avalon/imt/proc/imtconst.htm.

9. *R. v Bow Street Stipendiary Magistrate and Others, #Ex P. Pinochet Ugarte
(No. 3)* [2000] 1 A.C. 147, [1999] 2 All E R 97; available at
www.parliament.the-stationery-office.co.uk/pa/ld199899/ldjudgmt/
jd990324/pino2.htm.

10. Amnesty International, *The Pinochet Case-Universal Jurisdiction and the
Absence of Immunity for Crimes Against Humanity*, Report-EUR 45/01/99,

January 1999, United Kingdom, www.amnesty.org/ailib/aipub/1999/
EUR/44500199.htm.

11. *Attorney-General of Israel v. Eichmann* (1962) 36 Intl.L.R. 5, and for a
summary, see www.gwu.edu/jaysmith/Eichmann.html.

12. See the discussion by Lord Millett in *R. v Bow Street Stipendiary
Magistrate and Others, Ex P. Pinochet Ugarte (No. 3)*, www.parliament.the-
stationery-office.co.uk/pa/ld199899/ldjudgmt/jd990324/pino7.htm.
Though the Supreme Court of Israel did assert universal jurisdiction,
Israel also invoked a statute that was more specifically limited to Nazi
crimes against Jews. See Gary Bass, "The Eichmann Case," forthcoming
in a collection of papers from The Princeton Project on Universal
Jurisdiction, edited by Stephen Macedo.

13. *R. v Bow Street Stipendiary Magistrate and Others, Ex P. Pinochet Ugarte
(No. 3)*, www.parliament.the-stationery-office.co.uk/pa/ld199899/
ldjudgmt/jd990324/pino9.htm.

14. "Belgian Judge Visits Chad to Probe Crimes of Ex-Dictator Hissène
Habré," *Human Rights News,* February 2002, www.hrw.org/press/2002/
02/habre0226.htm; see also "The Case Against Hissène Habré," *Human
Rights Watch Web,* www.hrw.org/justice/habre/.

15. Princeton Project on Universal Jurisdiction, *The Princeton Principles on
Universal Jurisdiction,* Program in Law and Public Affairs, Princeton
University, Princeton, N.J., 2001.

16. *The Princeton Principles on Universal Jurisdiction,* p. 49, n. 20.

17. Clyde Haberman, "Israel Is Wary of Long Reach in Rights Cases," *New
York Times,* 28 July 2001, p. A1.

18. Reuters, "Ruling Likely to End Sharon's War Crimes Case," *New York
Times,* 15 February 2002, p. A8; Myint Zan, "Crimes against Humanity:
'Immunity' vs 'Impunity,'" *Korea Times,* 8 March 2002,
www.koreatimes.co.kr/kt_op/200203/t2002030817202048110.htm.

19. "Bush Urged to Support World Court," *New York Times,* 17 July 2001.

20. Juliet Eilperin, "House Approves U.N. Payment Legislation Would
Provide $582 Million for Back Dues," *Washington Post,* 25 September
2001, p. A01.

21. David Sanger, "President Defends Military Tribunals in Terrorist Cases,
New York Times, 30 November 2001, p. A1; Neil Lewis, "The Military
Tribunals: Rules on Tribunal Require Unanimity on Death Penalty,"
New York Times, 28 December 2001, p. A1.

22. International Commission on Intervention and State Sovereignty, *The Responsibility to Protect*, International Development Research Centre, Ottawa, 2001. Available at www.iciss-ciise.gc.ca.

23. I. Kant, *Perpetual Peace: A Philosophic Sketch*, Second Supplement, www.mtholyoke.edu/acad/intrel/kant/kant1.htm.

24. John Stuart Mill, "A Few Words on Non-Intervention," in John Stuart Mill, *Essays on Politics and Culture*, Gertrude Himmelfarb, ed., Anchor Books, New York, 1963, p. 377 (first published in *Fraser's Magazine*, December 1859). For further discussion, see Michael Doyle, "The New Interventionism," *Metaphilosophy* 32/1–2, January 2001.

25. L. Oppenheim, *International Law*, vol. 1, Longmans, Green & Co., New York, 1948 (first published 1905), p. 279; my italics.

26. Michael Walzer, *Just and Unjust Wars*, Penguin, Harmondsworth, 1980, p. 107.

27. Some of the criticism can be found in the lectures by Michael Ignatieff and Tzvetan Todorov in Nicholas Owen, ed., *Human Rights, Human Wrongs—Oxford Amnesty Lectures 2001*, Oxford University Press, Oxford, 2002.

28. Michael Walzer, "The Argument about Humanitarian Intervention," *Dissent*, Winter 2002, pp. 29–37.

29. Michael Walzer, "The Politics of Rescue," *Dissent*, vol. 42, Winter 1995, p. 36; "The Argument about Humanitarian Intervention," p. 29.

30. Walzer, *Just and Unjust Wars*, pp. 53–54, 86, 89.

31. Walzer, "The Politics of Rescue," p. 36.

32. James D. Steakley, *The Homosexual Emancipation Movement in Germany*, Arno Press, New York, 1975, p. 110.

33. Kofi Annan, "Two Concepts of Sovereignty," *The Economist*, 18 September 1999, www.un.org/Overview/SG/kaecon.htm.

34. Convention on the Prevention and Punishment of the Crime of Genocide, UN General Assembly 260A(III), 9 December 1948, www.unhchr.ch/html/menu3/b/p_genoci.htm.

35. Rome Statute of the International Criminal Court, Article 7, www.un.org/law/icc/statute/romefra.htm.

36. *The Responsibility to Protect*, pp. xi–xii and p. 32, par. 4.19.

37. Press Release SG/SM/7136 GA/9596, Secretary-General Presents His Annual Report to General Assembly (20 September 1999), http://srcho.un.org:80/Docs/SG/index.html.

38. Brad Roth, *Governmental Illegitimacy in International Law,* Clarendon Press, Oxford, 1999, p. 324.

39. General Assembly Resolution 2625 (XXV), Annex, 25 UN GAOR, Supp., no. 28, UN Dec A/5217 (1970), at 121, www.fletcher.tufts.edu/pens/2625.htm; also cited in Roth, pp. 161–162.

40. Security Council Resolution 688, 5 April 1991, http://srcho.un.org:80/Docs/scres/1991/688e.pdf. I owe this and the following two examples to Gregory Fox, "The Right to Political Participation in International Law," in Cecelia Lynch and Michael Loriaux, eds, *Law and Moral Action in World Politics,* University of Minnesota Press, Minneapolis, 1999, p. 91.

41. Security Council Resolution 794, 3 December 1992, http://srcho.un.org:80/documents/sc/res/1992/s92r794e.pdf.

42. Security Council Resolution 841, 16 June 1993, http://srcho.un.org:80/Docs/scres/1993/841e.pdf.

43. The thesis goes back to Kant's *Perpetual Peace,* section II, and is also associated with Joseph Schumpeter. See Michael Doyle, "Liberal Institutions and International Ethics," in Kenneth Kipnis and Diana Meyers, eds., *Political Realism and International Morality,* Westview, Boulder, Colo., 1987, pp. 185–211; first published as "Liberalism and World Politics," *American Political Science Review,* 80:4, 1986, pp. 1152–1169. There are many discussions of the thesis on the web; see, for example, http://users.erols.com/mwhite28/demowar.htm.

44. "In the Treaty's Words: 'International Stability'," *New York Times,* 17 July 2001, page A8.

45. *The Responsibility to Protect,* p. xi, pp. 12–13, paragraphs 2.7–2.15, and pp. 47–50, paragraphs 6.1–6.18.

46. This objection was pressed by John Broome when I gave an earlier version of this paper as an Amnesty Lecture at the University of Oxford. My response partially reflects comments made by Nir Eyal, who was also present on that occasion.

47. The preceding paragraph owes much to Leif Wenar's thoughtful comments.

48. Speech to SS Leaders in Posen, 4 October 1943, cited in Karl Dietrich Bracher, *The German Dictatorship,* Praeger Publishers, New York, 1971, p. 423.

49. Michael Doyle, "Liberal Institutions and International Ethics," in Kipnis

and Meyers, *Political Realism and International Morality*, p. 220. See this paper generally for a discussion, with many contemporary illustrations, of some of the consequentialist aspects of humanitarian intervention.

50. Tzvetan Todorov, "Right to Intervene or Duty to Assist?" in Nicholas Owen, ed., *Human Rights, Human Wrongs—Oxford Amnesty Lectures 2001*, Oxford University Press, Oxford, 2002.

51. For further discussion of the basis of ethics see my *Practical Ethics*, second edition, Cambridge University Press, Cambridge, 1993, chapter 1, or R. M. Hare, *Moral Thinking*, Oxford University Press, Oxford, 1981.

52. See Alvin Gouldner, "The Norm of Reciprocity," *American Sociological Review*, 25:2, 1960, p. 171.

53. For references, see Leonard Swidler, ed., *For All Life: Toward a Universal Declaration of a Global Ethic*, White Cloud Press, Ashland, Oreg., 1999, pp. 19–21.

54. Swidler, ed., *For All Life*, pp. 29–36.

55. See Samuel Huntington, *The Clash of Civilizations and the Remaking of World Order*, Simon & Schuster, New York, 1996.

56. Quoted from Erskine Childers, "Empowering the People in Their United Nations," a speech given at a symposium on "The United Nations at Fifty: Creating a More Democratic and Effective UN," Hesburgh Centre for International Studies, University of Notre Dame, 2 December 1994, www.globalpolicy.org/resource/pubs/childer1.htm. For a contemporary defense of the same idea, see George Monbiot, "Let the People Rule the World," *The Guardian*, 17 July 2001, available under the heading "Globalisation" at www.monbiot.com.

5 one community

1. David Barstow and Diana B. Henriques, "Gifts for Rescuers Divide Terror Victims' Families," *New York Times*, 2 December 2001.

2. Joyce Purnick, "Take the Cash. You're Making Us Look Bad," *New York Times*, February 11, 2002, p. B1; Nick Paumgarten, "Free Money: Trumpery Below Canal," *The New Yorker*, 18 and 25 February 2002, p. 58; Joyce Purnick, "For Red Cross, a New Round of Complaints," *New York Times*, February 21, 2002, p. B1.

3. For a summary see www.unicef.org/media/sowc02presskit/. The full report is also accessible from this page.

4. Purnick, "Take the Cash. You're Making Us Look Bad," p. B1.

5. Henry Sidgwick, *The Methods of Ethics,* seventh edition, Macmillan, London, 1907, p. 246.

6. Heinrich Himmler, speech to SS leaders in Poznan, Poland, 4 October 1943; cited from www.historyplace.com/worldwar2/timeline/ Poznan.htm.

7. R. M. Hare, *Freedom and Reason,* Clarendon Press, Oxford, 1963; *Moral Thinking,* Clarendon Press, Oxford, 1981.

8. William Godwin, *An Enquiry Concerning Political Justice and Its Influence on General Virtue and Happiness,* first edition, first published 1793, edited and abridged by Raymond Preston, Knopf, New York, 1926, pp. 41–42.

9. "Famine, Affluence and Morality," *Philosophy and Public Affairs,* 1:2, 1972, pp. 231–232.

10. See, for example, Raymond D. Gastil, "Beyond a Theory of Justice," *Ethics,* 85:3, 1975, p. 185; Samuel Scheffler, "Relationships and Responsibilities," *Philosophy and Public Affairs,* 26:3, 1997, pp. 189–209, reprinted in Samuel Scheffler, *Boundaries and Allegiances,* Oxford University Press, Oxford, 2001, pp. 97–110; Samuel Scheffler, "Conceptions of Cosmopolitanism," *Utilitas,* 11:3, 1999, pp. 255–276, reprinted in *Boundaries and Allegiances,* pp. 111–130. Note, however, that while Scheffler argues against what he calls "extreme cosmopolitanism" and insists that we have "underived special responsibilities" to those close to us in various ways, he does not take a position on whether we have special responsibilities to our compatriots, as compared to those in other countries. (See *Boundaries and Allegiances,* p. 124.) For an excellent discussion of the extensive literature on this topic, see Darrel Moellendorf, *Cosmopolitan Justice,* Westview, Boulder, Colo., 2002, chapters 3–4.

11. Samuel Parr, *A Spital Sermon,* preached at Christ Church upon Easter Tuesday, 15 April 1800, to which are added notes. J. Mawman, London, 1801.

12. Galatians vi:10.

13. Parr, *A Spital Sermon,* p. 4.

14. Nel Noddings, *Caring: A Feminine Approach to Ethics and Moral Education,* University of California Press, Berkeley, 1986, p. 86; for a related passage see also p. 112.

15. William Godwin, *Memoirs of the Author of a Vindication of the Rights of Woman,* ch. vi., p. 90, second edition, quoted in William Godwin,

Thoughts Occasioned by the Perusal of Dr Parr's Spital Sermon, Taylor and Wilks, London, 1801; reprinted in J. Marken and B. Pollin, eds., *Uncollected Writings (1785–1822) by William Godwin,* Gainesville, Fla.: Scholars' Facsimiles & Reprints, 1968, pp. 314–315. As K. Codell Carter notes (op cit, p. 320, fn) the passage italicized in the original is from Terence (*Heautontimorumenos,* I. 77), and is usually translated as "nothing human is alien to me." Godwin's argument for the importance of "individual attachments" is reminiscent of Aristotle's discussion of the need for friendship in his *Nicomachean Ethics,* Book IX, sec. 9.

16. R. M. Hare, *Moral Thinking: Its Levels, Method and Point,* Clarendon Press, Oxford, 1981, Part I.

17. See Yonina Talmon, *Family and Community in the Kibbutz,* Harvard University Press, Cambridge, Mass., 1972, pp. 3–34.

18. See Martin Daly and Margo Wilson, *The Truth About Cinderella: A Darwinian View of Parental Love,* Yale University Press, New Haven, 1999.

19. Bernard Williams, "Persons, Character and Morality," in Bernard Williams, *Moral Luck,* Cambridge, Cambridge University Press, 1981, p. 18.

20. See, for example, W. D. Ross, *The Right and the Good,* Clarendon Press, Oxford, 1930, p. 21.

21. See p. 111, above.

22. M. Rosenzweig, "Risk, Implicit Contracts and the Family in Rural Areas of Low-Income Countries," *Economic Journal,* 98, 1988, pp. 1148–1170; M. Rosenzweig and O. Stark, "Consumption Smoothing, Migration and Marriage: Evidence from Rural India," *Journal of Political Economy,* 97:4, 1989, pp. 905–926. I am grateful to Thomas Pogge for this information.

23. Michael Walzer, *Spheres of Justice,* Basic Books, New York, 1983, p. 12.

24. Eamonn Callan, *Creating Citizens: Political Education and Liberal Democracy,* Clarendon Press, Oxford, 1997, p. 96. This and the following quotation are cited from Melissa Williams, "Citizenship as Identity, Citizenship as Shared Fate, and the Functions of Multicultural Education," forthcoming in Walter Feinberg and Kevin McDonough, eds., *Collective Identities and Cosmopolitan Values,* Oxford University Press, Oxford, 2002.

25. Walter Feinberg, *Common Schools/Uncommon Identities: National Unity and Cultural Difference,* Yale University Press, New Haven, 1998, p. 119.

26. Benedict Anderson, *Imagined Communities: Reflections on the Origin and Spread of Nationalism,* Verso, London, revised edition, 1991, p. 6.

27. Robert Goodin, "What Is So Special about Our Fellow Countrymen?" *Ethics,* 98, 1988, p. 685; and reprinted in Robert Goodin, *Utilitarianism as a Public Philosophy,* Cambridge University Press, Cambridge, 1995, p. 286. I was reminded of this quotation by Christopher Wellman, "Relational Facts in Liberal Political Theory: Is There Magic in the Pronoun 'My,'" *Ethics,* 110:3, 2000, pp. 537–562.

28. Goodin, *Utilitarianism as a Public Philosophy,* p. 286.

29. Wellman, "Relational Facts in Liberal Political Theory," pp. 545–549; the third point is also made by David Miller, *Principles of Social Justice,* Harvard University Press, Cambridge, Mass., 1999, p. 18.

30. Karl Marx, *Wage Labour and Capital,* in David McLellan, ed., *Karl Marx: Selected Writings,* Oxford University Press, Oxford, 1977, p. 259.

31. John Rawls, *The Law of Peoples,* Harvard University Press, Cambridge, Mass., p. 120.

32. John Rawls, *A Theory of Justice,* Oxford University Press, London, 1971, p. 12; see also p. 100.

33. Rawls, *The Law of Peoples,* p. 40.

34. Rawls, *The Law of Peoples,* p. 117.

35. Rawls, *The Law of Peoples,* p. 106.

36. For further details, see Rawls, *A Theory of Justice,* pp. 4f, 453f.

37. Rawls, *The Law of Peoples,* p. 108.

38. Rawls, *The Law of Peoples,* p. 116; for references to the work of Beitz and Pogge, see Chapter 1, note 13, above.

39. Leif Wenar, "The Legitimacy of Peoples," in P. de Greiff and C. Cronin, eds., *Global Politics and Transnational Justice,* MIT Press, Cambridge, Mass., 2002, p. 53.

40. All figures are from the Organization for Economic Cooperation and Development. Figures on the overall fall in aid from developed countries are from the 2001 Development Co-operation Report, Statistical Annex, table 14; figures for individual nations come from charts under the heading "Aid at a Glance by Donor." These tables and charts are available at www.oecd.org.

41. World Bank, *World Development Indicator 2001,* table 6.8, www.worldbank.org/data/wdi2001/pdfs/tab6_8.pdf.

42. Organization for Economic Cooperation and Development, Documentation, Statistical Annex of 2001 DCR, Table 13, available at webnet1.oecd.org/EN/document/0,,EN-document-59–2-no-1–2674–0,FF.html.

43. See Bureau of Labor Statistics, U.S. Department of Labor, *Consumer Expenditure Survey 1999,* Current Aggregate Expenditure Shares Tables, for example Table 57, www.bls.gov/cex/1999/Aggregate/age.pdf.

44. Vernon Loeb and Bradley Graham, "Tough Choices Skirted? Pentagon Critics Say Bush's Proposed Increase Blunts Drive to Reform the Military," *Washington Post,* 10 February 2002, p. A06.

45. Elizabeth Bumiller, "Bush Plans To Raise Foreign Aid and Tie It To Reforms," *New York Times,* 15 March 2002, p. A8.

46. Rowan Scarborough, "'Peace Dividend' Apparently Paying Off," *Washington Times,* 9 March 1998, p. A4.

47. Program on International Policy Attitudes, *Americans on Foreign Aid and World Hunger: A Survey of U.S. Public Attitudes,* 2 February 2001, www.pipa.org.

48. World Bank, News Release 2002/212/S, 21 February 2002, "World Bank Estimates Cost of Reaching the Millennium Development Goals at $40–60 Billion Annually in Additional Aid," http://lnweb18.worldbank.org/news/pressrelease.nsf/673fa6c5a2d50a67852565e200692a79/81e7fb4c3d8bba3f85256b660067b411?OpenDocument; see also "The Costs of Attaining the Millennium Development Goals," a summary of a World Bank Policy Research Working Paper by Shantayanan Devarajan, Margaret J. Miller, and Edward G. Swanson, at www.worldbank.org/html/extdr/mdgassessment.pdf.

49. The 2000 U.S. census estimated that there were 209 million Americans over the age of 18. See U.S. Census Bureau, *2000 Census of Population and Housing, Profiles of General Demographic Characteristics,* May 2001, table DP-1, www.census.gov.

50. Peter Unger, *Living High and Letting Die,* Oxford University Press, New York, 1996, p. 136–139.

51. The question is raised by Leif Wenar, "What We Owe to Distant Others," presented at the Global Justice Conference, Center for Law and Philosophy, Columbia Law School, New York, 31 March–1 April 2001. See also David Crocker, "Hunger, Capability and Development," in William Aiken and Hugh LaFollette, eds., *World Hunger and Morality,*

second edition, Upper Saddle River, N.J., Prentice Hall, 1996, pp. 211–230.

52. World Bank, *Assessing Aid: What Works, What Doesn't, and Why,* Oxford University Press, Oxford, 1998, p. 1; available at www.worldbank.org/research/aid/aidpub.htm.

53. World Bank, *Assessing Aid: What Works, What Doesn't, and Why,* p. 14.

54. World Bank, News Release 2002/228/S, 11 March 2002, "Now More Than Ever, Aid Is a Catalyst for Change: New Study Shows Effects of Development Assistance over Last 50 Years," http://lnweb18.worldbank.org/news/pressrelease.nsf/673fa6c5a2d50a67852565e200692a79/865e6e90a8a6f97f85256b790050c57c?OpenDocument#paper. An executive summary of the research paper, "The Role and Effectiveness of Development Assistance" is available at the same web address.

55. World Bank, *Assessing Aid: What Works, What Doesn't, and Why,* p. x.

56. Alberto Alesina and David Dollar, "Who Gives Foreign Aid to Whom and Why?" NBER Working Paper 6612, pp. 22–23. Available at www.nber.org/papers/w6612.

57. See, for example, Arthur van Diesen, *The Quality of Aid: Towards an Agenda for More Effective International Development Co-operation,* Christian Aid, London, 2000; available at www.christian-aid.org.uk/indepth/0004qual/quality1.htm.

58. Sidgwick, *The Methods of Ethics,* pp. 489–490.

59. See, for example, John Cassidy, "Helping Hands: How Foreign Aid Could Benefit Everyone," *The New Yorker,* 18 March 2002, p. 60.

60. Elizabeth Bumiller, "Bush Plans To Raise Foreign Aid and Tie It To Reforms," *New York Times,* 15 March 2002, p. A8.

6 a better world?

1. Cited from W.-T. Chan, *A Source Book in Chinese Philosophy,* Princeton University Press, Princeton, N.J., 1963, p. 213. I owe this reference to Hyun Höchsmann.

2. Attributed to Diogenes by Diogenes Laertius, *Life of Diogenes of Sinope, the Cynic.* The same remark is attributed to Socrates by Plutarch, in *Of Banishment.*

3. John Lennon, *Imagine,* copyright © 1971 Lenono Music.

4. Branko Milanovic, *Worlds Apart: The Twentieth Century Promise That Failed,* work-in-progress, www.worldbank.org/research/inequality.

5. On this and other ideas about the nature of global institutions, see Daniel Weinstock, "Prospects for Global Citizenship," a paper read to the Global Justice Conference, Center for Law and Philosophy, Columbia Law School, New York, 31 March –1 April 2001. Weinstock argues persuasively against some common objections to the idea of global citizenship.

6. For one model, see Sam Daws and Frances Stewart, *Global Challenges: An Economic and Social Security Council at the United Nations.* A report sponsored by Christian Aid, London, 2000, www.christian-aid.org.uk/indepth/0006unec/unecon1.htm.

index